W9-DFK-164

To Asia,
With
Love

To Asia, With Love

Hetty McKinnon
雷瑜

Prestel

Munich London New York

A note on the photography

When I had the idea for *To Asia, With Love*, I imagined a book that not only conveyed nostalgia, but also captured a strong sense of home. Hence, it just felt right that I would take the photos myself.

I am not a professional photographer, but the act of taking photos was ingrained in me from a very young age. My father was an avid amateur photographer and always had cameras lying around the house. He took a lot of photos, developed film in a makeshift darkroom in our laundry and always traveled with a huge camera case. One of my favorite childhood memories is sitting in a dark room as he projected home movies onto our walls. I inherited many of his cameras, and one of my most treasured possessions is his Nikon FE, which I still use in my everyday photography.

All the food photos in this book were taken on 35 mm or medium format film, and are unfiltered and largely unedited. Film delivers a nuance, a timeless elegance and honesty that is almost impossible to replicate in digital photography. Film is evocative, it invites the viewer into the frame and it makes us *feel*.

All the photos were taken at my home in Brooklyn. The surfaces are predominantly my kitchen bench, my dining table, my side table and my coffee table. The forks, knives and spoons are all my own, and the bowls, plates, tablecloths and linen are not props, but are from my personal collection. The mess in the kitchen is also real, and the hands are those of my children, who are always in the real-time act of eating when the photo is taken—they are never waiting for me to perfect the frame. It's not always pretty, but it's my real life.

A new, green frontier for Asian(ish) food

There are many misconceptions when it comes to Asian food. Many believe that the ingredients are intimidating, that Asian flavors are hard to achieve at home, or that Asian food is "meaty." This book will dispel all these myths and more.

While meat does feature heavily on Asian restaurant menus, Asian home cooking is much more balanced and actually leans more heavily on the side of greens. Traditionally, meat was rationed and a luxury in Asian homes. The stir-fry is a great example of "meat-rationing," making the meal go further with the inclusion of ample greens. On these pages, my aim is to democratize Asian food, showing home cooks how to create big-flavored vegetarian (and often vegan) Asian dishes, featuring lots of vegetables and always made using the simplest of everyday ingredients.

Over the years, I've met many readers who have commented that they would eat Asian food every day if they knew how to make it. *To Asia, With Love* will show home cooks how easy it can be to achieve healthy, bright Asian flavors using ingredients you can find at your local supermarket. While there are a handful of ingredients that may require a trip to the Asian grocer (or a few clicks online), most of the ingredients are basic and easy to find.

The recipes in this book are accessible, familiar and comforting, but will also challenge you to think differently about the possibilities of cooking modern Asian flavors at home.

Embracing
a third culture

I was culturally confused for most of my life. I didn't understand who I was, until I started to cook. In food, I found the connection to my cultural identity that I'd been searching for my entire life.

My parents immigrated to Australia from Guangdong province, a coastal region of southeast China, which borders Hong Kong and Macau. In the early 1960s, they married in Sydney and moved out to a Victorian semi-detached house in the south-western suburbs, where my siblings and I grew up, and where my mother and brother still live today. At the time, we were one of three Chinese families on the street—the other two families were my aunt, uncle and cousins who lived right next door, and my other aunt and grandmother who lived on the corner. At home, we were a typical Chinese immigrant family—my siblings and I spoke Cantonese to our parents and English to one another, and Chinese customs and traditions were observed with reverence. My mother cooked constantly, and at times it felt like food was her way of staying connected to her distant motherland. For breakfast, she served hearty savory meals—fried rice, macaroni soup and noodles, which we devoured while watching our favorite cartoons. Dinnertime was sacred in our house—every night at 5 pm, just as the closing credits of *Gilligan's Island* or *The Brady Bunch* rolled on the television, my mother would holler "sikh fan" (literally "eat rice" in Cantonese, but the phrase actually means to "eat dinner"), summoning her children to the table. We ate a traditional Chinese banquet every night—soup, followed by an array of stir-fried meats and greens, served alongside bowls of white rice.

Growing up, I was not always comfortable with my identity. Even though I was born in Australia, I didn't particularly feel Australian, or Chinese for that matter. I was always teetering somewhere in between. I spent a lot of my childhood in a holding pattern, neither here nor there. As the children of immigrants, in many ways assimilation was our burden—we were the ones tasked with learning to co-exist in two worlds, to speak two languages, to translate for our parents, to write our own sick notes for school, to be the bridge between home and the outside world.

Assimilation was not a concept completely foreign to my parents. For school, my mother packed me a very "normal" lunch—Vegemite on white bread and an apple for snack. On Mondays we were allowed to order "party pies" from the school canteen (back then it was hard to purchase loaves of bread on Mondays because the commercial bakeries were closed on weekends). On the school playground I got a taste of what it was like to be a "true blue" Aussie.

After the birth of my third child, Huck, I started cooking in earnest, and this is when everything clicked into place. The more I cooked, the more connected I felt to my mother and her cultural heritage. When I was running my salad-delivery business, my mother would join me in the kitchen to provide advice (Chinese mothers love to give unwanted advice) and we talked all day. She would also bring me traditional Chinese ingredients like black fungus, lotus root or seaweed and not-so-gently hint at what an excellent salad ingredient they would be (she was always right too!). This time was seminal for me, allowing

Contents

Introduction

To Asia, With Love is my homecoming, a joyous return to all the humble yet deeply nurturing flavors and meals of my childhood. It is also a celebration of the exciting and delicious possibilities of modern Asian cooking.

The food that we grow up eating stays with us forever. My mother didn't work outside the home, but she was always busy. Her kitchen was constantly in motion—on the stove there would be tong (soup) bubbling away, jook (congee) simmering for lunch, and by the sink a tangle of greens sat in colanders, ready to be trimmed. Throughout the house there was always evidence of our next meal, or food for the future. In our laundry room there were huge jars of preserved eggs and pickling ginger, and salted pork and fish dangled under fine netting on a makeshift clothesline on the porch, alongside our washed clothes. All around the house there were crates of fruit, boxes of ma ma mian (our preferred brand of instant noodles) and no less than three freezers, brimming with pre-made dumplings, fried rice and wontons, ready to be thawed at a moment's notice for a delicious meal. As is often the case with immigrant cooks, my mother's food was unfussy and frugal. She never wasted food and even though she cooked a fresh meal for the family every night, she would often keep leftovers for her own lunch or dinner. She grew her own food in our suburban backyard—scallions, gourds, chiles, mandarins, kumquats and greens—and managed to create stunning meals from these humble ingredients. It is with this ethos that I have created the recipes in this book, showcasing big flavors achieved from minimal ingredients, using everyday vegetables.

Today, as I navigate the happy anarchy of raising three children, I find myself going back to the simple food of my youth. I yearn to recreate the same uncomplicated, colorful, soul-enriching Cantonese food for my own family. The memory of my childhood home, with the incessant scraping of my mother's wok chuan (spatula), the omnipresent thrum of her kitchen exhaust and the clatter of chopsticks and bowls as our table was set, are sounds that I want my children to hear as well.

The flavors in this book are not strictly Chinese, but they are Asian(ish). *To Asia, With Love* offers recipes that are rooted in the East, with hints of the West. The recipes are Asian in origin, but modern in spirit; they are inspired by tradition, with a global interpretation. Many of the recipes represent my exploration of my personal culinary roots as a Chinese girl born in Australia, and as an adult living between disparate cultures. Most importantly, this book is a celebration of how flavor can so powerfully connect us to our past and create pathways to our future.

me to delve deeper into my mother's life beyond being my mother. I saw her humor, her tenacity and her wisdom. I saw her in me, and me in her. Cooking alongside my mother allowed me to understand the confluence of culture, how we can be a mixture of a lot of things and still exist in harmony.

While many of the recipes in this book are very traditional, others are not. Although I love to explore the foods that I grew up eating, there is a rebellious side of me that often feels a strong pull to dismantle these traditions and create new ones. You will see examples of this in the dumplings chapter of the book; while I adore traditional Chinese dumplings, at my home you're more likely to find my family eating dumplings filled with spinach and feta than water chestnuts or napa (Chinese) cabbage. The way I cook is, in many ways, third-culture cooking, a cross-pollination of ideas and techniques that are grounded in my Chinese heritage, yet greatly influenced by growing up in the Western world. It is not distinctly Chinese, nor Australian, but rather a third interpretation of the two cultures.

How to cook Asian food, any day of the week, with everyday ingredients (and a few notes on how to use this book)

Asian food offers many layers of flavor, which may taste complex, but are actually easily achieved at home on any day of the week. Asian food is everyday food. The meals I grew up eating—stir-fried greens, stews, noodles, rice—were all basic foods made with unfussy ingredients. In recent years, as I have explored the foods of my heritage and embarked on learning to cook them myself, while also adapting them to my vegetarian diet, I have discovered techniques, shortcuts and tricks that make cooking Asian food at home a lot more simple.

Load up your "Asian" pantry

I have said this many times before: your pantry is your ultimate not-so-secret weapon in creating incredible weeknight meals. If you cook often, chances are you'll already have most of the ingredients in this book in your pantry. Most people will have staples like soy sauce, sesame oil, rice vinegar and coconut milk. I also use a lot of tahini in my Asian cooking—it's a worthy substitute for Chinese sesame paste, which is also made of toasted sesame seeds. Always have a few varieties of noodles on hand—rice noodles, egg noodles, wheat noodles, mung bean vermicelli (just to name a few) are dried and keep indefinitely. If I'm at the supermarket or an Asian grocer, I will often buy fresh noodles that I will freeze when I get home (they don't have to be thawed, just drop the frozen noodles straight into a pot of salted boiling water).

Explore umami

The secret to tasty food is umami. Known as the "fifth taste," umami translates to "pleasant savory taste" or "deliciousness" in Japanese. Umami foods include soy sauce, sesame oil, fermented black beans, shiitake mushrooms, seaweed and miso—basically, the ingredients that make food delicious. I encourage you to use this book to explore the world of umami, playing with these everyday foods in your daily cooking.

Oodles of noodles

For the noodle dishes in this book, don't get too caught up in the type of noodle specified. The noodles in my recipes are the *ideal* type but not the *only* type that can be used. Just use whatever you have on hand, and perhaps buy some different varieties next time you're shopping. The noodle recipes in this book are an excellent reason to load up your pantry with a range of dried noodles.

Nice rice

Growing up, we only ate one type of rice—SunRice brand white long grain. As a result, I'm not overly fussy about the type of rice we eat. Use what you have. I have even made fried rice with leftover basmati rice, with pleasing results. For an everyday grain, I recommend Koshihikari rice, an extremely versatile Japanese-style short-grain rice. It retains moisture longer, has lovely separated grains and is also great for sushi or onigiri. Also, pay special attention to recipes that call for "glutinous rice" (also known as "sticky" or "sweet" rice)—this is a very different type of rice, which needs to be soaked before cooking, and will break down when cooked and become gluey.

The good oil

Generally, I use a neutral oil like vegetable, sunflower or grapeseed oil in my Asian cooking. But sometimes I also use olive oil when the occasion, or lack of alternative, demands it. I am not overly strict when it comes to the type of oil I cook with, but I'm always aware that olive oil imparts a lot more flavor, so be conscious of this when you are preparing your food. Sesame oil is essential to Asian cooking, so always have some on hand to bring that special touch to a dish.

On heat

In previous books I've taken a restrained approach to chile, but in this book I've unleashed my inner spice fanatic. I am obsessed with chile and in recent years I have taken to topping almost every meal with chile oil, hot sauce or sliced fresh chile. But don't fret if you don't love chile— just add the level of spice you're comfortable with. I use the "everything oil" on page 25 in a lot of recipes (it's not called that for nothing), but if you don't like spice I encourage you to make my everything oil without the chile, thus turning it into an "aromatic oil." Even without the chile, the spices of ginger, garlic, star anise and cinnamon will impart a melodic liveliness to the oil.

Make it vegan

While writing this book, I realized that our diet growing up was largely dairy free. My mother, having grown up in China, where dairy wasn't a part of her daily diet, is lactose intolerant and traditionally food from Southeast Asia just doesn't include much cream, cheese or milk. Eggs, however, are a huge part of Asian cooking. We ate a lot of eggs growing up—my mother's frizzled-edged wok-fried eggs, laced with soy sauce, are still comfort food for me. One of my earliest memories was my grandmother rolling peeled, hard-boiled eggs across my forehead after I fell and hurt my head (there is an old wives' tale that boiled eggs help bruises to heal).

In this book, I encourage you to "veganize" any recipes that do include dairy or eggs. In many cases this could be as simple as substituting with homemade cashew cheese or commercial vegan cheese—there are excellent vegan products on the market now, including sour cream, yogurt, feta, mozzarella, cream cheese and more. And, of course, there are many alternatives to dairy milk—coconut, oat and macadamia are a few of my favorite nondairy varieties.

The everyday Asian pantry

Honestly, there is not a lot of difference between your "everyday" pantry and your "Asian" pantry. We are so lucky to live in an age when the "international" aisles of our local supermarkets are so well stocked with ingredients, allowing us to easily create multicultural meals at home. Here are my essential Asian(ish) pantry items.

Black fungus

Also known as cloud ear or wood ear mushrooms, I prefer the simple name of black fungus. Like shiitake mushrooms, Chinese black fungus generally comes dried, so it must be rehydrated in hot water before use. You may be able to find it fresh but it's quite rare. Black fungus is a great absorber of flavor. In traditional Chinese cooking, it is most often used in stir-fries and braises, but I love its crinkly, crisp texture in salads. Black fungus is usually available from the international aisle of your supermarket, otherwise you'll find it at Asian grocers and online. It can be stored in an airtight container in a cool place for six months or longer.

Curry powder

There are many varieties of curry powder on the market, made with a different mix of spices. In Asian cooking, I prefer to use Malaysian curry powder, which is a blend of coriander seeds, cumin, fennel, cinnamon, cloves, black peppercorns and dried red chiles. I don't make my own curry powder at home—I usually use the store-bought Ayam brand, which is the one my mother uses, but any kind of mild curry powder will work.

Dried shiitake mushrooms

These are an essential pantry staple, a foundation ingredient in Chinese cooking. Dried shiitakes are potent in umami flavor, and the smell of them soaking in hot water and/or cooking takes me straight back to my childhood. They can be used in stews, braises, broths, dumplings and more. My mother would chop off the stems and add them to jook as a special treat for me—once cooked, they became thick and chewy and they were my favorite. To rehydrate, simply soak in hot water for 20–30 minutes, though you can leave them for longer to get them really plump if you have the time. And remember, don't throw that rehydrating water away—keep it for stock or for flavoring the finished dish (just make sure you strain it to remove any sediment). Dried shiitake mushrooms can be easily found at most supermarkets nowadays—store them in an airtight container in a cool place for six months or longer.

Fermented black beans

Fermented black beans (dou chi) will require a trip to the Asian grocer (or a few clicks online), but they are totally worth the effort. They add such incredible flavor to stir-fries and salad dressings. For vegans especially, fermented black beans are life-changing, delivering an intense, delicious flavor (make sure you try my black bean Caesar dressing on page 185). Fermented black beans are made from dried and salted soybeans and are sold in bags at Asian grocers. At home, store them in an airtight jar in your pantry and they will last for months. When cooking, make sure you rinse them first to reduce some of the strong saltiness. I have a recipe for homemade black bean sauce in this book (see page 143), which I highly recommend you make. Of course, if you can't locate fermented black beans, commercial black bean sauce is a worthy substitute (though it does have a lot more additives).

Gochugaru

Gochugaru is ground Korean chile, with a texture that is part flake, part powder. It imparts a gentle heat, with a hint of sweetness, smokiness and fruitiness. It is used in kimchi but also in soups, stews and chile oil. You may need to visit an Asian grocer (or look online) to find gochugaru and if you do, buy a big bag, as it keeps well in an airtight container. If you can't find it, you can substitute with regular chile flakes or cayenne pepper, but you'll need to reduce the quantities greatly, because gochugaru is nowhere near as spicy.

Gochujang paste

Synonymous with Korean food, gochujang is a vibrant red spicy paste that is also salty and a little sweet. Made with chile, glutinous rice, fermented soybeans and salt, it has a thick, sticky texture, and is commonly used in marinades and sauces, and to add flavor to rice, soups and broths. I love using gochujang (diluted with olive oil or yogurt) as a spice rub for vegetables, or as a condiment with roasted vegetables, fried eggs and rice.

Kecap manis

Kecap manis is a sweet, syrupy, caramelly soy sauce from Indonesia. It is particularly great for creating intense flavors and adding sweetness. In Australia, it is relatively easy to find in the international aisle at major supermarkets. In other parts of the world, kecap manis can be harder to locate in everyday supermarkets, so you may need to visit an Asian grocer or buy online. If you see a product called "sweet soy sauce" (Kikkoman makes one, but there are other brands too), this is very similar to kecap manis and can be used as a substitute. If you can't find kecap manis, make your own by combining 1 tablespoon of dark soy sauce with 1 tablespoon of soft dark brown sugar, honey or maple syrup.

Kimchi

Kimchi is a Korean staple of salted and fermented vegetables—usually napa (Chinese) cabbage or radish—seasoned with gochugaru, ginger and scallion. Kimchi is also an important part of daily banchan (side dishes), which are served with every Korean meal. While I often make my own (see my recipe for a quick kimchi on page 38), there are also many great store-bought varieties. If you are vegetarian, make sure you opt for a vegan kimchi as many commercial brands contain fish sauce. Kimchi is such a versatile item to have in your fridge—I use it in fried rice, tacos, sandwiches, noodles, in practically everything. And it is also good for you—kimchi is fermented, so it contains "healthy bacteria" called lactobacillus, which aids digestion.

Kimchi

Maggi Seasoning Sauce

Maggi is my magic elixir, the sauce from my childhood that makes everything taste better. As a child, we only really got to have Maggi with our jook, but now, as an adult, I shamelessly leave it out on my dining table—a small splash on eggs, jook, soup or noodles brings the magic. Maggi is more than soy sauce—it has more umami and it's more delicious. Though ubiquitous in Asia, Maggi originally comes from Switzerland and is eaten in many countries around the world—from Africa to the Middle East and Mexico. In fact, there are many variations, and in some countries they are spicy or more garlicky. Maggi is available at most supermarkets. Just make sure you don't substitute Maggi for soy sauce as it is not the same thing; use it sparingly—just a few drops on your finished dish goes a long way.

Mirin

This sweet rice wine is a staple in Japanese cooking, used to make marinades, teriyaki sauce or to finish Japanese soups, including miso soup. For me, it is also essential for Asian-inspired salad dressings. Mirin is similar to sake but has less alcohol and a higher sugar content—the sugar occurs naturally during the fermentation process so it does not contain any added sugar. Mirin is often referred to as "sweetened sake." If you can't find mirin at your market, you can make a good substitute by adding ½ teaspoon of sugar to every 1 tablespoon of dry white wine or rice vinegar.

Miso

Miso is an essential source of salty, earthy and funky flavor. Made of fermented soybeans and koji (a mold that's also used to make sake), there are many varieties of miso that differ depending on how long they have been left to ferment—the longer the fermentation, the darker and more complex in flavor miso becomes. In regular supermarkets you will usually find two different varieties: white (shiro) miso is mellow in flavor and is usually the type I choose, while red (aka) miso has a much more intense taste. Sometimes you may find yellow (shinshu) miso, which is somewhere in the middle in terms of flavor and color. There are also varieties of miso made with chickpeas, barley and brown rice.

Rice vinegar

Rice vinegar (sometimes labelled rice wine vinegar) is an essential ingredient in Asian salad dressings. It is less acidic than white vinegar and has a mild, delicate flavor with just a hint of sweetness. Seasoned rice vinegar has small amounts of sugar and salt added, perfect for sushi rice or salad dressings.

Seaweed

Allow me to wax lyrical about seaweed for a moment. Seaweed is
one of the world's most sustainable and nutritious foods. I have long
believed seaweed to be the future of food because of how few resources
it needs to grow—it is a zero-input food, meaning it does not require
fresh water, fertilizer, feed or arable land to thrive. It readily absorbs
dissolved nitrogen, phosphorus and carbon dioxide directly from the
sea and reproduces at a phenomenal rate—it can grow as much as an
inch (2.5 centimeters) a day. It also contains more calcium than milk,
more vitamin C than orange juice, and more protein than soybeans. In
fact, fish do not naturally produce omega-3 fatty acids; they obtain these
nutrients by eating seaweed. I love seaweed, but I do acknowledge it can
still be difficult to find or expensive to purchase. Because of this, I have
minimized the number of seaweed-centric recipes in this book, but I
do encourage you to include more seaweed in your life. There are many
types of dried seaweed—wakame and kombu are both great for salads
and also for making Japanese dashi stock. Seaweed is also rich
in umami. In fact, in 1908, chemistry professor Kikunae Ikeda at the
Tokyo Imperial University identified the glutamic acid in kombu
seaweed as umami, the fifth taste. I often add seaweed to soups or
homemade stocks to amp up the flavor. If you can't find dried seaweed
at your local supermarket, stock up on your next trip to the Asian grocer
or buy it online.

Sesame oil

For me, a drop of sesame oil makes just about every dish better,
imparting an umami-rich deliciousness. There are two types of sesame
oil: regular, untoasted sesame oil is made from raw seeds and is
generally considered better for cooking; toasted sesame oil has a richer,
more intense flavor and is often used in the final stages of cooking or
when serving. To make my life easier, and to maximize pantry space,
I only ever use toasted sesame oil. Some say it becomes bitter when
cooked over high heat, but I've never noticed this myself. Popular
opinion says that a little bit of toasted sesame oil goes a long way, but I
don't mind using a brave splash for a more assertive flavor.

Sesame seeds

Sesame seeds add an earthy nuttiness to dishes. White seeds have a more
delicate flavor, while black sesame seeds have a stronger aroma, which
works really well in desserts. The seeds are available either toasted or
untoasted. Being a lazy-ish cook, I usually buy the toasted variety to
save on one step of the cooking process. To toast raw seeds, pour them
into a large frying pan and place over low heat; move the seeds around
constantly using a pair of wooden chopsticks or a wooden spoon until
they are golden. Allow to cool, then pour them into a jar for storage.

Shaoxing rice wine

Shaoxing rice wine (also spelled shaohsing) is fermented from glutinous
rice and does contain some wheat, so it is not gluten free. Shaoxing
rice wine is an important ingredient in traditional Chinese cooking.

My mum always had a bottle by her wok for stir-fries, deglazing or for braising meats and fish. I love to use shaoxing rice wine to add a rich, aromatic quality to marinades or sauces. If you don't have any, substitute with dry sherry or simply omit.

Soy sauce, tamari, liquid aminos and coconut aminos

It may surprise some, but I am very undisciplined when it comes to soy sauce and I don't particularly have a favorite brand. I use soy sauce, tamari, liquid aminos and coconut aminos interchangeably. I've always had a variety of "soy sauces" in my pantry, but nowadays I tend to stick with tamari, liquid aminos and coconut aminos, which are all gluten free. Traditional soy sauce contains wheat, and is slightly more salty and darker in color, but essentially all these sauces taste the same. In the past, Asian cuisine was difficult for sufferers of celiac disease or those with wheat intolerances because of the pervasive use of soy sauce, but when cooking at home it is now very easy to substitute with these gluten-free alternatives. Dark soy sauce is not essential, but it does come in handy when you are looking for a deeper color or or a less salty, more sweet addition to your meals. In Chinese, dark soy sauce is called lǎo chōu, meaning aged, which perfectly sums up the richer, slightly thicker quality of this variety.

Sriracha and other chile sauces

A trip to the Asian grocer will reveal hundreds of chile sauces, with each country or region in Asia offering their own unique variety. Growing up, my mother always had Koon Yick brand chile sauce in the fridge—it is not the spiciest sauce, but it provides a nice, bright heat to most dishes (this is the kind you often find at Cantonese restaurants or at dim sum). I also like Sriracha, a chile sauce with a healthy kick of garlic.

Tahini

Some may be surprised by how extensively tahini is featured in this book—I use it as a substitute for Chinese sesame paste (ji ma jiang), a thick paste made from roasted sesame seeds. The texture is much thicker than tahini, closer to the feel of peanut butter, but since it's hard to find in regular supermarkets, I am happy enough with the results I get from using tahini instead. Of course, if you are at the Asian grocer, pick up a jar of sesame paste to experiment with the slightly heavier consistency. I always opt for hulled tahini (made from seeds that have the exterior coating removed), as it is smoother and less bitter.

Tamarind

Made from the pulp from tamarind tree pods, tamarind is most often used in stir-fries or noodle dishes to give that kick of pleasant sourness. Tart yet sweet, it is often the secret ingredient in pad thai noodles. For ease, I prefer to use tamarind purée, which is tamarind paste that has already been diluted. Tamarind can also be purchased in a block, which is more like pulp. This needs to be diluted in warm water.

All about chile oil

I have loved spicy food ever since I was a child. When I go to a Chinese restaurant, I ask for the chile sauce even before I sit down. Adding a hot sauce or oil to my Asian food has become my ritual. Here are two of my favorite chile oils—everything oil (my homemade version of Sichuan chile oil) and rayu (a Japanese-style spicy sesame oil). If you only have one chile oil for the rest of your life, it must be everything oil. As the name suggests, I add it to everything, and I hope you will too.

I know many home cooks don't love chile as much as I do. Of course that is fine, but I encourage you to add a tiny bit of heat to suit your preferred level of spice. It's all about finding the balance that works for you.

Everything oil
MAKES ABOUT 2 CUPS (500 ML)

This is my version of Sichuan chile oil (sometimes called mala hot sauce), which I have called "everything oil" because, well, it makes everything taste better. Like my ginger–scallion oil (see page 28), it can be used as a salad dressing, a stir-fry sauce, a dumpling dip or simply as a topping. Such is my passion for this oil, you will see it as an ingredient in many recipes in this book because it hits all the right notes—heat, spice, salt, umami—without needing to reach for too many ingredients. The Sichuan peppercorns leave a slight numbing and tingly feeling in your mouth. If you don't care for this sensation, or can't get hold of Sichuan peppercorns or gochugaru, then just use red chile flakes instead (you may need to reduce the quantity, though, as chile flakes are spicier).
    This oil definitely gets better with time. The longer it sits, the more flavorful and aromatic it becomes.

A note for those who don't love spice: make this oil without the chile flakes, or use a dramatically reduced amount. The oil will still be aromatic from the ginger, garlic, star anise and cinnamon, and a worthy addition to *everything* you eat.

2 tablespoons red chile flakes
2 tablespoons Sichuan peppercorns
2 tablespoons gochugaru (Korean red chile flakes)
1 tablespoon sea salt
1 cup (250 ml) vegetable or other neutral oil
2-inch (5 cm) piece of ginger, peeled and finely chopped
4 garlic cloves, finely chopped
2 star anise
1 cinnamon stick

In a heatproof bowl, add the chile flakes, Sichuan peppercorns, gochugaru and sea salt.

Place the oil, ginger, garlic, star anise and cinnamon in a small saucepan over medium–high heat for 3–4 minutes—the oil is ready when it looks thin, like water. Remove from the heat and very carefully pour the hot

>

oil into the bowl with the spices—the oil will sizzle and spit, so stand back. Allow to cool.

Stir before serving. I don't strain it as the chile and spices continue to flavor the oil over time. Everything oil can be drizzled over noodles, dumplings, soups and salads. Store in a sterilized jar (no need to refrigerate) for up to 3 months.

Rayu

MAKES ABOUT ½ CUP (125 ML)

Rayu is an aromatic sesame oil from Japan, often served with ramen or gyoza (Japanese dumplings). Because rayu is made with sesame oil, it has a heavier, more robust finish, so a few drops is usually enough. I like to add it to noodle soups, salads, jook, fried eggs, or any dish that benefits from a bit of spice. If you can't find gochugaru, which is mildly spicy, use regular red chile flakes, but reduce the quantity depending on the spiciness of your brand of flakes.

2 tablespoons gochugaru (Korean red chile flakes)
1-inch (2.5 cm) piece of ginger, peeled and finely chopped
2 garlic cloves, finely chopped
2 scallions, white parts only, finely chopped
½ cup (125 ml) toasted sesame oil

Place the gochugaru in a small heatproof bowl.

In a small saucepan over medium–low heat, add the ginger, garlic, scallions and 3 tablespoons of the oil. Bring to a gentle simmer, then reduce the heat to low and cook for 3–4 minutes, swirling the pan often, until the ingredients turn golden (be careful not to let them burn!).

Pour the hot oil over the chile flakes. Add the remaining oil and stir to combine, then allow the oil to cool to room temperature. At this point, you can strain the mixture and pour the clarified oil into a glass jar or you can simply pour the oil, sediment and all, into a jar and allow the chopped ingredients to settle at the bottom. Store in a sterilized jar (no need to refrigerate) for up to 3 months.

Other essential sauces and oils

Ginger–scallion oil

MAKES ABOUT 2 CUPS (500 ML)

You'll find many uses for ginger–scallion oil in this book. It is particularly pleasing as a salad dressing, tossed through soba noodles, used as a dipping sauce for scallion pancakes or dumplings, or folded through roasted vegetables. You can also do as I did as a child and slather it over white rice.

All ginger–scallion oil recipes vary on the ginger–scallion sliding scale—some are ginger-heavy, while others are scallion-centric. Mine is the former, and decidedly so. Some people like to grate their ginger to make it finer and smoother, so do this if this is your preference also. For me, I like to taste my ginger emphatically, so I chop it into a fine dice.

5 ounces (140 g) ginger, peeled and finely chopped (a roughly 7-inch / 17.5-cm piece)
6 scallions, finely sliced, white and green parts separated
1 tablespoon tamari or gluten-free soy sauce
2 teaspoons sea salt
1¼ cups (310 ml) vegetable or other neutral oil

Place the ginger, white part of the scallion, tamari or soy sauce and sea salt in a heatproof bowl.

Place the oil in a small saucepan over medium–high heat for 3–4 minutes. It is hot enough if it sizzles when you place a wooden chopstick into it. Very carefully pour the oil over the ginger and scallion mixture. Allow to cool, then add the green part of the scallion and stir to combine. Store in an airtight container in the fridge for several weeks. Bring to room temperature before using.

Vegan "fish sauce"

MAKES ABOUT ¾ CUP (185 ML)

I have been making this "fish sauce" at home for years, to use in pad thai, larb and salads. I'm not sure if it is really possible to exactly mimic the sweet, salty, fishy and funky quality of real-deal fish sauce, but this vegan offering comes pretty close. You could also add a touch of pineapple juice for an extra layer of funkiness.

½ cup (125 ml) lime juice
2 tablespoons brown sugar
2 tablespoons tamari or soy sauce
1 small garlic clove, grated
½ teaspoon sea salt

Whisk together all the ingredients in a small bowl until the sugar has dissolved. Store in an airtight container in the fridge for up to 4 weeks.

Reliable dumpling dipping sauce

MAKES ½ CUP (125 ML)

This is a great all-rounder dipping sauce, perfect for serving alongside dumplings, scallion pancakes, or as a slightly sweet salad dressing.

¼ cup (60 ml) tamari or soy sauce
2 tablespoons maple syrup
1-inch (2.5-cm) piece of ginger, peeled and finely chopped
1 scallion, finely sliced
2 teaspoons toasted white sesame seeds
2 teaspoons toasted sesame oil

Whisk together all the ingredients in a small bowl. Store in an airtight container in the fridge for up to 2 weeks.

Asian greens

Greens are as central to an Asian meal as rice. Growing up, it was simply unthinkable to serve dinner without a bowl of stir-fried or braised greens. Cooked at high temperatures in a sizzling wok (or frying pan), Asian vegetables came to the table vibrantly green on the plate, and tender-crisp to the bite.

Nowadays, Asian greens like bok choy, gai larn (Chinese broccoli) and choy sum are widely available at supermarkets. For the recipes in this book, instead of specifying a particular type of Asian green, I suggest you use whichever variety you have on hand or prefer. They are interchangeable and can all be used in similar ways.

And don't worry if you can't find Asian greens; just use broccoli, broccolini or even kale. Gai larn, in particular, tastes very similar to broccoli. When shopping for Asian greens, look for vibrant green leaves without any wilted or yellow leaves or dark spots. And wash them well to remove any dirt and sediment. If you ask my mum, she would advise you to wash them at least three times (I wash them once). Once washed, drain to remove the excess water and use within 1–2 hours so they don't become soggy.

From left to right: napa cabbage, baby bok choy, Shanghai baby bok choy, ong choy and gai larn

These are some of my favorite Asian greens

Bok choy means "white vegetable," referring to the color of the stem, and there are various types available. Full-sized bok choy has a thick white stem with dark-green leaves and I have found that it is interchangeable with chard. I generally prefer to use baby bok choy as the leaves are sweeter and more tender. There are two varieties of baby bok choy: the "dwarfed" variety, which basically looks like a miniature version of the full-sized green; and the more ubiquitous variety with a pale-green stem (sometimes called Shanghai baby bok choy).

Choy sum is similar in appearance to gai larn (Chinese broccoli), but it is a lighter green and the stalks are thinner and less robust. Choy sum literally means "vegetable heart"—the leaves are very tender and cook in almost no time. When I'm making noodle soups or broths, I usually add these greens after removing the pot from the heat as the residual heat is enough to wilt the leaves.

Gai larn (Chinese broccoli) is one of the most popular and widely available Asian greens. With a dark leaf and thick stalk, it has a slightly bitter taste that is similar to broccoli (char it the same way as you do broccoli—so delicious). In a salad, try replacing broccoli or broccolini with gai larn for variety. I usually slice my stalks in half so they cook faster; you can separate the leaves and stalks and cook the stalks for 20–60 seconds longer than the leaves, but honestly, I enjoy my stalks really crisp, so I usually toss them in the pan together.

Ong choy is the Asian green with the most names: water spinach, water morning glory, river spinach, kangkong . . . This green is not widely available in everyday supermarkets, but since it's my favorite Asian green of all time, I wanted to tell you about it. Ong choy is unique—it has long, hollow stems, which stay quite crunchy when cooked, and mild, tender leaves, which become sweet and creamy. The texture of cooked ong choy is like no other. It is traditionally stir-fried with garlic, chile and fermented soybean paste (or shrimp paste). If you find this green at your Asian grocer, try the recipe on page 163. Substitute with spinach if you can't find ong choy.

Wombok is also known as napa cabbage (or Chinese cabbage in some parts of the world). It is widely available in most supermarkets. The stem and leaves are pale green and tender, which makes them perfect for enjoying raw in salads.

Things to go with everything

How to make a perfectly jammy egg

I never thought I would include instructions for how to cook the perfect boiled egg, but since this is a skill I have only recently mastered myself, I wanted to share it. For many years, I was cooking eggs haphazardly, not really keeping an eye on timing or when I added the egg to the water. Now I pay much more attention and the result is perfect jammy eggs, every time.

What are "jammy" eggs, you may ask? They are that sweet spot between a soft- and a medium-boiled egg; that point when the yolks have *just* solidified and become velvety. Jammy is how I prefer my eggs, but sometimes I will cook them for 6 minutes to get a runnier yolk. For a slightly harder yolk, opt for 8–9 minutes.

To make perfect jammy eggs, bring a deep saucepan of water to the boil. Place your eggs (I never remember to bring my eggs to room temperature for boiling, so I always use them straight from the fridge) into the boiling water, and immediately set your timer for 7 minutes. When the timer goes off, drain them straight away and run under cold water; keep the water running until the eggs are completely cold (alternatively, submerge them in an ice bath).

Note: These instructions are for large (2 ounce / 60 g) eggs.

Marinated eggs, three ways

Each of these marinating liquids will uniquely color the eggs. In the case of the beet and soy eggs, the color will start at the outer part of the egg white and slowly move its way towards the yolk, depending on how long you leave them in the pickling liquid.

Soy eggs
MAKES 4

¾ cup (185 ml) tamari or soy sauce
1½ teaspoons five-spice powder
2 scallions, roughly sliced
⅓ cup (80 ml) mirin
2 teaspoons rice vinegar
4 boiled eggs, cooked to your liking, peeled

In a saucepan, combine the tamari or soy sauce, five-spice powder, scallion, mirin, rice vinegar and 1 cup (250 ml) of water. Bring to the boil over medium heat, then reduce the heat and simmer for 2 minutes. Add the eggs, then remove from the heat and allow to sit for 1 hour. You can leave the eggs marinating in the soy mixture, kept in the fridge, for up to 1 week.

Beet-pickled eggs

MAKES 4

1 large beet, peeled and sliced
1 cup (250 ml) apple cider vinegar
⅓ cup (75 g) sugar
1 teaspoon sea salt
4 boiled eggs, cooked to your liking, peeled

In a saucepan, add the beet and 1½ cups (375 ml) water. Cover and cook over medium–low heat for 20 minutes or until the beet is soft. Add the vinegar, sugar and sea salt and stir until the sugar has dissolved. Remove from the heat and allow to cool.

Place the eggs in a medium jar. Pour the beet mixture into the jar and top with a couple of beet slices to weigh down the eggs.

Cover and pickle in the fridge for 2 days before eating, though you can leave them for up to 2 weeks if you like.

Note: I have found that using juice from canned beets provides a more vibrant crimson color. If you want brighter eggs, drain the juice from two small cans of beets (save the beets for another use) and cook with the vinegar, sugar, salt and water as above.

Marbled tea eggs

MAKES 4

⅓ cup (80 ml) soy sauce
2 tablespoons dark soy sauce (optional)
3 bay leaves
1 teaspoon five-spice powder
1 teaspoon sea salt
2 black teabags
4 boiled eggs, cooked to your liking, unpeeled

In a saucepan, combine the soy sauces, bay leaves, five-spice powder, sea salt, teabags and 1½ cups (375 ml) of water. Bring to a simmer over medium heat, then reduce the heat and simmer, covered, for 5 minutes. Remove the pan from the heat and allow the liquid to cool completely, then discard the teabags.

Place an egg in the palm of your hand and, using the back of a spoon, gently crack the shell all over, enough to allow the marinade to penetrate the egg white and create a marbled pattern. Repeat with the remaining eggs, then return them to the marinade and leave for at least 12 hours, though maximum marbling will occur at around 24 hours.

You can leave the eggs marinating in the soy mixture, kept in the fridge, for up to 1 week.

Scallion pancakes
MAKES 8

The perfect scallion pancake is a multi-layered delight—crispy, flaky and light. Made with a technique similar to laminated pastries like croissants and puff pastry, the key to flaky pancakes is building layers, which puff up and separate during cooking.

Like dumplings, scallion pancakes are made with hot water dough, where the just-boiled water breaks down the gluten in the flour, creating an incredibly pliable dough that doesn't bounce back as much, and is easier to roll out. And because it has such low gluten development, you can work with it straight out of the fridge.

Serve the scallion pancakes with your choice of dipping sauce.

2 cups (300 g) all-purpose flour, plus extra for dusting
¾ cup (185 ml) just-boiled water, cooled for about 2 minutes
Vegetable or other neutral oil
1 shallot, very finely diced
2 tablespoons toasted sesame oil
2 scallions, finely chopped
Sea salt
Reliable Dumpling Dipping Sauce (see page 29), Ginger–Scallion Oil
    (see page 28), Everything Oil (page 25), soy sauce or black vinegar,
    to serve

You can use a food processor to mix the dough, but I prefer to do it by hand. Set a heatproof bowl on a tea towel (to stop it from moving around) and add the flour and 1 teaspoon of sea salt. Using a wooden spoon or a pair of chopsticks, stir the flour as you slowly pour in the just-boiled water, a little at a time. Continue stirring until it comes together. Turn out the dough onto a floured work surface and knead for 5 minutes, until the dough is smooth (the dough will initially be quite hot so be careful; it cools down quickly as you work it). Transfer to a bowl, cover with a damp tea towel or plastic wrap and allow it to rest at room temperature for 30 minutes. At this stage, you could also put your dough in the fridge and roll it the next day. I often do this.

Meanwhile, heat a small frying pan over medium heat. Add a small drizzle of oil, then toss in the shallot and cook for 2 minutes or so, until soft. Set aside.

Flour your work surface. Divide the dough into eight equal pieces and roll each into a smooth ball. Cover the dough balls with a damp tea towel so they don't dry out. Working with one ball at a time, roll it out into a disc roughly 6 inches (15 cm) in diameter. Using a pastry brush, paint a thin layer of sesame oil over the dough. Starting from one end, roll the dough into a thin cylinder, then wind it into a coil, tucking the end underneath. Cover with a tea towel and continue with the remaining dough balls.

The next step creates more layers in the pastry. Gently flatten the coiled dough with the palm of your hand, then re-roll it into a 6-inch (15 cm) disc, making sure you flour the surface and rolling pin often so the dough doesn't stick. Again, brush with a layer of sesame oil, then sprinkle lightly with the shallot and scallion, along with a pinch of sea salt. Roll up into a cylinder again and wind into a coil. Flatten and then roll out into a into a 6-inch (15 cm) disc. Set aside and cover with a damp tea towel. Repeat with the rest of the dough.

Heat a frying pan over medium–high heat and, when hot, add a drizzle of vegetable oil. Slip one disc into the pan, reduce the heat to medium and cook, shaking the pan and flipping the pancake often, until golden and crispy on both sides. This should take 2–3 minutes. Transfer to a plate lined with a paper towel to absorb any excess oil. Repeat with the remaining discs. When cool enough to handle, cut into wedges and serve with your favorite sauce.

Quick kimchi

This kimchi paste can be used for long fermentation or for quick-pickled vegetables, which can be eaten almost immediately. While I am no expert on kimchi making, this method is based on a recipe I learned in a kimchi class I attended many years ago, where the teacher presented two unique ways to enjoy kimchi. One was an okra kimchi, which had been fermented for more than 12 months, and was brimming with the deep, funky flavors one would expect from a long bout of pickling; the second was fresh purslane leaves, gently coated in the kimchi paste. These leaves were not fermented at all, and the kimchi paste was used as more of a salad dressing on the fresh, crispy leaves. I'd never tasted fresh "kimchi" before and, needless to say, I was very excited by the idea.

With this paste recipe in hand, allow yourself to experiment with different vegetables and combinations. The general principle of kimchi making—salt first, rinse, coat in paste—can be applied to most vegetables that can be eaten raw (what I'm saying is, this method won't work with, say, potatoes!). I love to pickle cucumber, radish, peach, even watermelon. Think of kimchi-ing as a great way to use up any leftover veggies you know you won't get through. Below are some ideas on vegetables that I like to pickle with this paste. I usually store my kimchi in the fridge; it keeps well for up to 2 weeks.

Lastly, in case you haven't heard, kimchi is good for you! It has vitamins and good bacteria, and enhances the immune system. Keep a jar in the fridge for whenever you need a healthy snack.

Kimchi paste

MAKES 1½ CUPS (360 g)

3 dried shiitake mushrooms
1 cup (250 ml) boiling water
1 teaspoon vegetable stock powder or sea salt
½ cup (50 g) gochugaru (Korean red chile flakes)
5 garlic cloves, sliced
½-inch (1.25 cm) piece of ginger, peeled and sliced
½ onion or 1 shallot, roughly chopped
1 apple, peeled, cored and roughly chopped

Soak the shiitake mushrooms in the boiling water for 30 minutes, then squeeze them out into the soaking water. Keep the mushrooms for another use (they can be stored in the fridge or freezer until you need them). Strain the mushroom water to remove any grit, then stir in the stock powder or sea salt until dissolved.

In a food processor or blender, add the gochugaru, garlic, ginger, onion or shallot, apple and mushroom water and whiz into a paste. Your kimchi paste is ready! See opposite for ideas on how to use it.

Daikon radish

1 pound (450 g) daikon or 1 bunch of radishes, finely sliced

2 tablespoons sea salt

2 scallions, finely sliced

2–3 tablespoons Kimchi Paste (see opposite), or more to taste

Mushroom

7 ounces (200 g) mushrooms (such as oyster, shimeji, shiitake or cremini),
smaller ones torn, larger ones sliced

2 teaspoons sea salt

2 scallions, finely sliced

2–3 tablespoons Kimchi Paste (see opposite)

Fennel

1 pound (450 g) fennel, finely sliced and fronds reserved

2 tablespoons sea salt

2 scallions, finely sliced

2–3 tablespoons Kimchi Paste (see opposite), or more to taste

In a large bowl, add your choice of vegetables (the above are suggestions, you could also use other vegetables too) and sprinkle over the specified quantity of sea salt. Massage the salt into the vegetables until they start to soften. Set aside for 30–60 minutes (if you are using larger leaves like napa (Chinese) cabbage, leave for about 1–2 hours). When ready, rinse the vegetables under running water (to remove most of the salt), then squeeze out the brine. Allow to drain well, then pat dry and place in a bowl.

Add the scallion and enough kimchi paste to coat the wilted vegetables and to suit your preferred level of spice, and stir through. Eat immediately or spoon into a sterilized jar and store in the fridge for up to 2 weeks.

Fresh leafy kimchi salad

SERVES 2 AS A SIDE, OR 1 PERSON WHO WANTS TO EAT A HUGE BOWL OF LEAVES

3½ ounces (100 g) salad leaves (watercress, purslane, pea shoots, baby spinach
or a combination)

2–3 tablespoons Kimchi Paste (see opposite)

2 tablespoons sunflower seeds

1 avocado, sliced into wedges

1 scallion, finely sliced

Handful of cilantro leaves

Juice of ½ lime or lemon

Extra-virgin olive oil or toasted sesame oil

Sea salt and black pepper

Place the leaves in a bowl and add enough kimchi paste to suit your preferred level of spice. Add the sunflower seeds, avocado, scallion and cilantro and season with sea salt and black pepper. Toss gently to combine. Finish with a squeeze of citrus and some oil, then serve immediately.

Kimchi Paste (opposite) and Fresh Leafy Kimchi Salad (above)

A ig
breakfast

The morning feast

In Western countries, you most likely start the day with a light meal of cereal, oatmeal, toast or eggs. In Asian culture, there is no holding back. When the day begins, it's game on.

Growing up, I didn't understand my mother's elaborate morning feasts. Because I'd never lived in Asia and witnessed such breakfast rituals, my Western upbringing steered me to believe that eating fried rice or noodles for breakfast was abnormal and just another of my mother's "Asian-mum idiosyncrasies." While I always appreciated my mother's feasts, there were mornings when I just longed for a bowl of cornflakes.

My mother started every day in the kitchen with conviction and purpose. Pots and wok on the stove, cleaver at the ready. My mother rarely missed an opportunity to deliver an epic meal. For breakfast, she served noodles, fried rice, jook (congee) and her Asian take on a cheese toastie—white bread dotted with tiny squares of char siu pork and finely chopped scallions, with Kraft cheese melted over the top. One of her signature breakfast dishes was macaroni soup, small pasta shapes floating in chicken or vegetable broth, speckled with shiitake mushrooms, peas, carrots and Spam (try my version of this dish on page 63). Yes indeed, Spam was frequently served at our family table and, honestly, I have fond memories of all my mother's canned meat dishes—she would pan-fry it until golden around the edges or steam it on top of rice, allowing the fragrant Spam juices to soak into the rice. For much of my childhood, there was nothing better than a Spam and fried egg sandwich for breakfast, the egg expertly frizzled in my mother's wok, complete with molten yolks. Cheese and Spam jaffles (similar to toasties) were another breakfast highlight, featuring the double-win of salty hot meat paired with salty, oozy processed cheese.

As I got older and spent more time in Asia, I realized that the grand breakfast feast was a big part of Asian culture. When I visited Singapore as a teenager, I became obsessed with the curry rice vermicelli from the breakfast buffet. Traditional breakfast dishes in Asia range from region to region, and many have their origins in street food, nabbed by hungry locals on their way to work. Dim sum is still my favorite breakfast of all.

Tomato and egg "shakshuka"

SERVES 4
GLUTEN FREE

Ice cubes

4 beefsteak tomatoes
(about 22 ounces / 615 g)

Extra-virgin olive oil

1-inch (2.5 cm) piece of ginger, peeled
and finely chopped

1 onion, sliced into thin wedges

¼ cup (30 g) brown sugar

4 large eggs

Handful of cilantro leaves,
roughly chopped

2 scallions, finely sliced

Sea salt and white pepper

Everything Oil (see page 25),
to serve

Bread, to serve (optional)

This is a classic hybrid dish, a clashing of cultures with spectacular results. Two loves combined—Chinese tomato and egg, a dish I tolerated growing up but now adore as an adult, reworked as a shakshuka. The recipe is an unassuming showstopper, offering all the distinctive sweet umami flavor of the classic Chinese dish, but with a very different sensibility. Serve with bread (or dare I say, rice?) to mop up the tomatoey juices.

Set up a large bowl with ice and cold water—this is your ice bath for peeling the tomatoes. Bring a saucepan of water to the boil. Score a small "x" at the bottom of each tomato and add them to the boiling water until the skins wrinkle and split—this should take 1–1½ minutes. Remove from the water and drop them straight into your ice bath. Once the tomatoes are cool, lift them out of the water and peel away their skin. Chop the tomato flesh.

In a frying pan over medium–high heat, add a drizzle of olive oil, along with the ginger and onion; stir well and cook for 2 minutes. Add the tomato, then reduce the heat to medium–low and cook, covered, for 5 minutes. Add the brown sugar and a splash of water, and squash the tomato a little to break it up. Cover and cook for another 2 minutes.

Make four little indents in the tomato mixture and gently crack one egg into each hole. Season with sea salt and white pepper. Replace the lid and cook over low heat for 5–6 minutes, until the whites are just set. Scatter with the cilantro and scallions and serve with everything oil and bread, if using.

Substitute

Beefsteak tomatoes: 1 can whole peeled tomatoes (tomatoes only, omit the juice)

Use gluten-free bread for gluten free

Egg, pea and ginger fried rice

SERVES 4
GLUTEN FREE

---

4 large eggs, beaten

Vegetable or other neutral oil

1-inch (2.5 cm) piece of ginger, peeled and finely chopped

---

4 cups (740 g) cooked brown or white rice (or a combination), preferably chilled in the fridge overnight

---

1 tablespoon tamari or gluten-free soy sauce

---

2 cups (310 g) frozen peas

---

2 scallions, finely sliced

Sea salt and white pepper

Fried rice was one of my mother's signature breakfast dishes when I was growing up. Comforting and filling, it was the perfect breakfast to get me through dreary school mornings. My mum made a range of simple fried rice dishes, always with eggs, often with peas and sometimes using frozen "mixed vegetables" (you know, the packet with carrots, corn and peas). When I got older, she introduced me to ginger fried rice and this zesty version quickly became my favorite. Fried rice for breakfast is a great reason to have leftover rice in the fridge—freshly cooked rice works too, but make sure you cool it for an hour or so; otherwise the rice will get clumpy when fried. I love the toothsome, chewy quality of brown rice, but use whatever rice you have on hand.

Season the eggs with a good pinch of sea salt.

In a hot wok or large frying pan, heat 1 tablespoon of oil for just a few seconds, then pour in the beaten egg. Cook over medium–high heat for 10–15 seconds, allowing the bottom to set slightly, then turn the egg with a stainless-steel spatula until just set. Break up the egg slightly, then remove from the wok or pan and set aside.

Heat another big drizzle of oil in the wok or pan, add the ginger and fry for 20 seconds to flavor the pan. Add the rice, breaking it up with the spatula, and fry for about 2 minutes. Next, add the tamari or soy sauce, peas and a few big pinches of sea salt and toss well. Continue to stir-fry for 4–5 minutes until the peas are cooked, then add the egg and mix well. Cook for another minute or so until everything is heated through. Add a few turns of white pepper. Taste and season with a little more salt if needed.

Take the pan off the heat and stir through the sliced scallions. Serve immediately.

Substitute

Peas: diced carrot or corn

Veganize

Omit the egg

Soy sauce chow mein with a fried egg

SERVES 4

7 ounces (200 g) dried egg noodles

Vegetable or other neutral oil

4 large eggs

7 ounces (200 g) bean sprouts

2 scallions, finely sliced

2 tablespoons toasted white sesame seeds

Sea salt and white pepper

Sauce

1 tablespoon light soy sauce or tamari

1 tablespoon dark soy sauce

2 teaspoons toasted sesame oil

This simple chow mein dish is most commonly served at dim sum restaurants, where the noodles are fried on the spot in the traveling hot trolley. At home, this is a breakfast staple, made from scant pantry ingredients. I adore the addition of bean sprouts—I have vivid memories of my mum sitting in her cavernous armchair, diligently tailing each sprout (a step I usually skip because I lack her dedication). My mum also adds garlic chives, so when they are in season, throw in a handful for a distinct aromatic flavor. The dark soy sauce adds the signature caramel color to the noodles—if you don't have any, just use regular soy sauce or kecap manis. I've added a fried egg to amplify the breakfast feeling, but you could also serve it with your favorite marinated egg (see page 33) or go without.

Bring a saucepan of salted water to the boil. Add the noodles and stir to loosen them up. Cook according to the packet instructions until just tender, about 2–4 minutes, then rinse under cold running water until cold. Drain and set aside.

For the sauce, mix together all the ingredients with 3 tablespoons of water in a small bowl.

Heat a wok or frying pan over high heat. When hot, add a drizzle of oil, then crack in one egg. Reduce the heat to medium and fry the egg until the edges are frizzled, the white is set and the yolk is cooked to your liking. Season with a pinch of sea salt. Remove and repeat with the remaining eggs.

Place the wok or pan back over the heat and, when hot, add a drizzle of oil, along with the noodles. Fry for 1–2 minutes, then add the bean sprouts and the sauce. Toss well to coat the noodles thoroughly, about 2 minutes. Remove from the heat, season with white pepper and toss to combine.

To serve, top with fried eggs, scallions and sesame seeds.

Substitute

Dried egg noodles: 14 ounces (400 g) fresh noodles

Use rice vermicelli for gluten free

Veganize

Omit the egg

Hong Kong scrambled egg sandwich, with a side of milk tea

Australia Dairy Company will feature on most lists of essential places to eat in Hong Kong. This bustling, no-frills, fast-moving cafeteria is a traditional Hong Kong restaurant (cha chaan teng), specializing in steamed milk pudding, custard dishes, fluffy scrambled egg toast and strong milky tea. No matter what time you arrive, there will be a line, so join the queue and take in the diversity of the people waiting—elderly locals going about their day, people on their way to work, local teens posing for selfies and tourists like me who had heard about this place from friends. This cafeteria is not for the faint hearted—the service is gruff, the pace is harried and the all-Chinese menu is not very helpful for those who can't read Chinese characters. However, with lots of pointing and nodding and, in my case, badly spoken Cantonese, you'll soon be sitting in front of my idea of perfection: a plate of the most buttery, salty, creamy scrambled eggs, wedged between two thick slices of white bread, with a side of strong milky tea.

The milk tea in Hong Kong is robust and full-bodied. A nod to their colonial days, I liken it to British "builder's" tea. Sipping a hot cup of Hong Kong milk tea felt incredibly nostalgic—when I was young, my mum and my aunt Susanna would serve their tea in dainty teacups with matching saucers, fortified with a healthy splash of evaporated milk or sweetened condensed milk. Hong Kong–style milk tea is traditionally blended with two types of tea leaves—Ceylon and Pu Lei (Yunnan black tea), but for ease at home, I recommend two black teabags brewed for several minutes.

SERVES 1

2 slices of white bread (as thick as you can find!)

Salted butter, at room temperature, for spreading and pan-frying

2 large eggs

2 tablespoons evaporated milk

½ teaspoon tamari, soy sauce or Maggi Seasoning Sauce

Sea salt

Milk tea

2 strong black teabags

About 1¼ cups (310 ml) boiling water

¼ cup (60 ml) evaporated milk

3–4 teaspoons sugar, to your liking

For the milk tea, place the teabags in a small teapot and steep in the boiling water for 3–4 minutes (you can also place the teabags directly into a mug and cover with a plate or bowl). Pour the tea into a cup or mug and add the evaporated milk and sugar. Stir well and serve immediately. You could also serve this cold by adding ice cubes.

Meanwhile, place the bread on a cutting board and butter both slices.

In a small bowl, whisk together the eggs, evaporated milk and tamari, soy or Maggi and season with a good pinch of sea salt.

Melt a small knob of butter in a small nonstick frying pan over medium heat. Slowly pour in the egg mixture—allow the egg on the bottom to set for a minute or so before stirring (you want the eggs to be folded in ribbons rather than in chunks). Remove the egg from the pan and place straight onto the buttered side of a slice of bread. Sandwich with the other slice, then cut off the crusts with a sharp knife and serve.

Substitute

Evaporated milk in milk tea: 2 tablespoons sweetened condensed milk and omit the sugar

Condensed milk French toast

Hong Kong–style French toast is another cha chaan teng specialty— thick white bread spread with sweetened condensed milk, and topped with even more of the sticky sweet milk. Growing up, my mother always kept a little jug of condensed milk in the fridge (later, she introduced the tube of condensed milk, which became a permanent fixture in her fridge door), which she would drizzle on toast for breakfast. I remember being intrigued by her morning ritual, and for many years, I thought sweetened condensed milk toast was her own personal quirk. Visiting Hong Kong again after decades of absence opened my eyes to many things, one of them being that my mum's affection for milky sandwiches is actually a Hong Kong breakfast tradition.

SERVES 1

2 thick slices of white bread

2–3 tablespoons sweetened condensed milk

1 large egg

Salted butter, for pan-frying and to serve

Place the bread on a cutting board and drizzle one slice with about 1 tablespoon of the sweetened condensed milk. Sandwich the bread together.

Crack the egg into a bowl (large enough to fit the sandwich) and beat well. Dip the sandwich into the beaten egg, turning to coat both sides; allow the bread to sit in the egg until it soaks it all up.

Heat a small frying pan over medium heat, add a knob of butter and swirl it around to coat the base. Add the eggy sandwich and pan-fry on one side for a minute or so until golden, then flip over and repeat on the other side. Remove from the pan and place straight on a serving plate. Top with a knob of butter and drizzle with the remaining condensed milk. Allow the butter to melt over the bread and eat immediately.

Three jook toppings

MAKES ENOUGH TO SERVE 4

Kale chips and everything oil

4 cups (about 160 g) kale leaves, torn, washed and dried well

Olive oil

Everything Oil (see page 25)

Sea salt

Preheat the oven to 280°F (140°C).

Place the kale on a large sheet pan and drizzle with a little olive oil. Massage the oil into the leaves, then spread them out in a single layer and roast for 20–25 minutes, until the leaves are crispy. Remove from the oven and sprinkle with sea salt. Set aside to cool, then scatter the kale over the jook and finish with a drizzle of everything oil.

Five-spice shiitake mushrooms and sesame

Olive oil

5 ounces (140 g) shiitake mushrooms, sliced

½ teaspoon five-spice powder

2 tablespoons tahini, well stirred

1 tablespoon toasted white sesame seeds

1 scallion, finely sliced

Sea salt

Heat a drizzle of oil in a frying pan over medium heat. Add the mushrooms and cook, tossing, for 3–4 minutes until golden. Remove from the heat and season with five-spice powder and sea salt.

Top the jook with the mushroom and a drizzle of tahini, and finish with a sprinkling of sesame seeds and scallion.

Quick pickled carrot salad with mustard seeds

1 large carrot, coarsely grated

2 tablespoons roasted peanuts, crushed

Juice of ½ lime

1 teaspoon sugar

Handful of cilantro leaves, chopped, plus extra leaves to serve

1 tablespoon vegetable or other neutral oil

1 teaspoon mustard seeds

Sea salt

Toss together the carrot, peanuts, lime juice, sugar, cilantro and a pinch of sea salt.

Heat the oil in a very small saucepan over medium–high heat; once hot, add the mustard seeds, then cover immediately to allow them to pop. Once the popping stops, pour them over the salad and toss to combine. Adjust any seasonings. Top the jook with the salad and finish with extra cilantro.

Tomato macaroni soup and scrambled egg

When I was growing up we ate several dishes that I thought were really unusual and unique to my mother. Macaroni soup was one of them. Small pasta shapes swimming in chicken or veggie broth, flavored with shiitake mushrooms, peas, carrots and ham. Sometimes Spam was also in that bowl. To me, this didn't feel like a distinctly Chinese dish, so I assumed it was just something my mum made when she was short on time. I continued to think it was a family recipe until a *very* recent trip to Hong Kong, where I saw it on the breakfast menu at McDonald's and practically every other cafe and cha chaan teng menu. I was shocked. Only then did I realize it was actually known as "Hong Kong–style breakfast"; it dawned on me that I still had much to learn about my family culture.

At a cafe close to my hotel in Hong Kong, I ordered a variation of this dish—tomato soup brimming with macaroni pasta, topped with scrambled egg. My love for this dish was instant, inspiring a childlike wonder for a bowl full of textures and childhood memories, just with a little twist.

SERVES 4

10½ ounces (300 g) dried elbow macaroni (or other small pasta shape)

4 large eggs

Olive oil

1 scallion, finely sliced

Sea salt and white pepper

Tomato soup

Olive oil

1 small onion, chopped

1 garlic clove, chopped

1 (28-ounce / 800-g) can diced tomatoes

2 cups (500 ml) vegetable stock

¼ cup (60 ml) ketchup

1 teaspoon sugar

Sea salt and white pepper

Bring a saucepan of salted water to the boil. Add the pasta and cook according to the packet instructions until al dente, about 5–6 minutes. Drain and refresh under cold water.

For the tomato soup, heat a drizzle of oil in a saucepan over medium heat, add the onion and cook for 1–2 minutes until translucent. Add the garlic and stir for 30 seconds. Pour in the tomatoes and stock and cook for 4–5 minutes, until the mixture is simmering. Season with sea salt and white pepper. Using a stick blender (or regular blender/food processor), whiz until smooth. Stir in the ketchup and sugar, then taste and season again if needed.

Meanwhile, crack the eggs into a small bowl and beat well. Season with sea salt and white pepper. In a frying pan over medium–high heat, add a drizzle of oil. Slowly pour in the egg mixture and cook, gently stirring occasionally, for barely 60 seconds, until the egg is just set. Break up the egg into chunks and set aside.

To serve, place some macaroni in a bowl and cover with hot soup. Top with scrambled egg and scallion.

Substitute

Canned tomatoes: fresh tomatoes

Use gluten-free pasta for gluten free

Veganize

Omit the egg

Soba breakfast platter

As the sun rises in Tokyo, locals file into tiny restaurants for their morning noodles, slurping shoulder to shoulder. All kinds of noodle dishes are eaten for breakfast in Japan, but soba is a favorite, served either hot or cold, sometimes topped with tempura, grilled fish cakes or onsen tamago (soft-boiled egg). This recipe is inspired by the morning soba noodle ritual we came across in Tokyo—a seiro (bamboo tray) of cold soba noodles (best eaten cold to experience the true texture, flavor and aroma of the buckwheat), served with a dipping sauce and condiments on the side.

SERVES 4

14 ounces (400 g) soba noodles

Drop of white vinegar

4 large eggs

4 radishes, julienned

1 carrot, peeled into thin strips or shredded

2 Persian cucumbers, sliced into thin discs

2 sheets of toasted nori, sliced into strips

2 scallions, finely sliced

Sea salt

Dipping sauce

1 cup (250 ml) vegetable stock

2 tablespoons tamari or soy sauce

¼ cup (60 ml) mirin

1 teaspoon sugar

For the dipping sauce, combine all the ingredients in a small saucepan over medium heat. Bring to a gentle boil, stirring, then remove from the heat and set aside to cool.

Bring a saucepan of salted water to the boil, add the soba noodles and cook according to the packet instructions until al dente, about 4–5 minutes. Drain immediately and refresh under cold running water. (Alternatively, drain the noodles and place them in an ice bath.) When completely cold, drain again.

In a saucepan of simmering water, add a drop of vinegar. Break one egg into a small bowl and gently ease it into the water. Cook for 2 minutes, until the white is just firm. If you prefer your yolk firmer, cook for another minute or two. Using a slotted spoon, transfer the egg to a plate lined with a paper towel and allow to drain. Repeat with the remaining eggs.

Place a mound of noodles onto each serving plate and add the eggs, vegetables, nori and scallions alongside. Season the noodles and eggs with a pinch of sea salt. Pour the dipping sauce into little bowls and serve with the noodle platter.

Note: You can eat this dish as you wish—you could pour the dipping sauce over the noodles and veggies and eat it like a cold soup, or you could lift cold soba noodles and veggies, one mouthful at a time, and dip them into the sauce, slurping them up quickly.

Substitute

Soba: udon or somen noodles

Poached eggs: Marinated Eggs (see page 33)

Use 100% buckwheat soba noodles, rice vermicelli or glass noodles for gluten free

Veganize

Omit the egg

Miso oats with egg and avocado

SERVES 2

1 cup (100 g) old-fashioned rolled oats

4 cups (1 liter) vegetable stock

2 tablespoons white (shiro) miso

4 large eggs (see page 33 for marinated eggs)

4 scallions, finely sliced

1 avocado, sliced

1–2 tablespoons toasted black or white sesame seeds

Sea salt

I learned to make this dish as a teenager, when my mum was laid up with back problems, leaving me as the primary cook in the house. I'd never made jook before, so my mother talked me through how to make savory oats instead. I was instantly charmed by this quick and simple way of replicating jook, in a fraction of the time. This is now my lunch-for-one staple, swiftly thrown together and topped with an egg, avocado, kimchi or even leftover salad. Drizzle with everything oil (see page 25) or your favorite hot sauce if you like it spicy.

Place the oats in a saucepan, add the stock and bring to the boil. Reduce the heat to low and place the lid on slightly ajar, then cook for about 15 minutes, until the oats have reached a porridge consistency. Turn off the heat and gradually stir in the miso paste, a little at a time, until it has dissolved into the oats. Taste and season with salt if needed.

Bring a saucepan of water to the boil, then add the eggs. Set the timer for 6 minutes for soft yolks, 7 minutes for "jammy" eggs and 8–9 minutes for hard-boiled eggs. When your timer goes off, drain the eggs immediately and either rinse them under cold running water or place in an ice bath until they are completely cold. Peel and cut in half.

Ladle the oats into bowls and top with the boiled eggs, scallions, avocado and sesame seeds. Season with a small pinch of sea salt and serve immediately.

Substitute

Old-fashioned rolled oats: steel-cut oats

Boiled eggs: fried eggs

Use gluten-free oats for gluten free

Veganize

Omit the egg

Lucky
noodles

The pilgrimage, that wasn't

The first time I visited Hong Kong, I was five. It was our first big family vacation, my first time on a plane and the first time my parents had returned to their homeland since becoming Australian citizens.

That trip was a homecoming for my parents, as we visited the ancestral homes of their families in Guangdong. We made a detour to Macau, where my mother had lived briefly, and then visited the bustling metropolis of Hong Kong.

My memories of Hong Kong are foggy, at best. I recall the constant brushing of bodies as we walked down the street, crowded escalators and being crammed into a small electronics store as my parents bought us cassette players, so we could record our favorite songs off the radio. I remember visiting my great-aunt's cramped, high-rise apartment block, which overlooked a murky body of water. I remember countless meals with relatives, strangers who looked familiar.

Almost four decades later, I returned to Hong Kong for a work project, taking with me a spectrum of emotions and unreasonably high expectations. Even though I had never lived there, much of my mother's extended family were still in Hong Kong and there was an irrational part of me that expected it to feel like home. I saw my trip as a pilgrimage of sorts, a voyage to rediscover my cultural roots.

Every day after work, on the precipice of dusk, I went exploring. I took the train to Sham Shui Po and ate freshly steamed cheung fun (rice noodles) crouched in an alleyway with the locals. I wandered through Jordan, browsing Temple Street Night Market, joined the queue at Australia Dairy Company for their famed scrambled egg sandwiches, and ordered darn tarts (egg custard tarts) from a hole-in-the-wall bakery in Sheung Wan. Everywhere I roamed, I was searching, curiously seeking answers to unasked questions, desperately seeking a sense of belonging.

What I look for in life more than anything is connection. But in Hong Kong, I felt alienated, displaced. I could speak the language, but only barely, and certainly not well enough to feel authentic. On the outside I looked the part, but inside I felt like a phoney.

Early one evening, on my last night in Hong Kong, I returned to Wong Chuk Hang, a burgeoning hipster-ish industrial-slash-residential area on the southern tip of Hong Kong Island where I had been staying, in search of noodles. A colleague had told me about a Thai market close by. Eventually I stumbled upon Nam Long Shan Road Cooked Food Market, filled with scantily partitioned stalls all offering Thai food. I looped around the perimeter, scoping out the menus; as was often the case, the meat-free offerings were non-existent. I eventually retraced my steps to the noodle shop at the entrance, remembering a woman with a friendly face. I smiled and asked, sheepishly, in my best broken Cantonese, "Do you have any vegetarian noodles?" She looked at me, confused, and replied sympathetically, "There are no vegetarians in Hong Kong." I laughed, sardonically. Though inaccurate, her claim was the harshest kind of irony, almost tantamount to "you don't belong here." Seeing the disappointment on my face, she relented and assured me that she would sort something out. She told me to sit, and retreated to the makeshift kitchen. A short time later she emerged with a steaming plate of glistening pan-fried rice noodles, brimming with vegetables, no meat in sight. I sighed, feeling overwhelmed with gratitude and finding inordinate comfort in the simple dish before me. After ten days of searching, I had finally found a piece of home in Hong Kong, in this plate of noodles.

Noodle know-how

Noodles are universally loved and incomparably crave-worthy, so always keep a good variety of dried noodles in your pantry, or fresh noodles in your freezer, for delicious weeknight cooking. Here is a list of my favorite types of noodles, all of which are featured in this book.

Egg noodles are made of wheat flour and egg, with a signature yellow color. There are many varieties (and names) of egg noodles, which are usually sold fresh: wonton noodles, chow mein, hokkien and lo mein are all varieties of egg noodles. There are also many varieties of dried egg noodles, which you can identify by their golden color. Egg noodles are excellent in fried noodle dishes, soups and salads.

Glass noodles are also known as "sweet potato noodles" or "Korean glass noodles" and they are most famously used in the Korean dish, japchae. When cooked, these thick noodles become translucent, with a pleasing chew. They are made from sweet potato starch, so they are vegan and gluten free.

Green tea noodles are thin Japanese soba noodles that have been infused with green tea. They are sometimes called cha soba. The green tea gives them a lovely delicate green color and a subtle tea flavor, and they are often served chilled in summer. Green tea noodles are vegan.

Mung bean vermicelli are known by many names—cellophane noodles, bean threads, bean thread noodles, crystal noodles or glass noodles. When cooking, as soon as they become completely transparent they are ready. Even though they look delicate, they are actually quite robust and easy to handle. I love using mung bean vermicelli for salads, soups and braised dishes. They are made from mung bean starch and are vegan and gluten free.

Ramen noodles come from Japan and are traditionally served in broth, with a multitude of toppings. While fresh, chewy ramen noodles are undoubtedly the best, for everyday cooking I usually opt for the packets of instant "ramen" noodles; these are not really ramen noodles at all but rather "instant noodles" or "2-minute noodles," available from supermarkets and corner stores all over the world. We grew up eating 2-minute noodles and I am not ashamed to say that I love them, though I very rarely use the flavor sachet and oil that comes in the packet, opting instead for my own miso broth or the like. They are also great pan-fried.

Rice noodles come in many different shapes and thicknesses and are incredibly versatile. The thick rice noodles are used in Vietnamese pho or pad thai, while there are also thinner, finer types called rice sticks. The thinnest strands are called rice vermicelli. The key difference with rice noodles is that they need to be cooked just before serving—if you put cooked rice noodles in the fridge, they tend to go hard and will need to be heated up again to soften. Also, be careful not to overcook rice noodles, as they can break apart easily. Cook until just soft, then drain immediately. Asian grocers will also sell fresh rice noodles, which you can definitely use in place of dried ones. Rice noodles are vegan and gluten free.

Soba noodles are traditionally made of buckwheat flour, however most commercial soba noodles we find at the supermarket will contain some wheat flour too. They are brown-ish in color, with an earthy flavor that makes them perfect for salads. If you are using them for salad, my tip is to cook them the night before or a few hours prior, rinse them until cold, then drizzle with oil to prevent sticking and put them in the fridge to firm up. Freshly cooked soba tend to be very soft and break up easily. If you're gluten-intolerant, look for 100 percent buckwheat soba. All soba noodles are vegan.

Somen noodles are white Japanese noodles made of wheat flour and they are very thin. They cook quickly, in about 3–4 minutes. Somen noodles are traditionally served cold, with a dashi dipping sauce (if you'd like to try a chilled noodle recipe, see page 105), but I also use them in warm soups. Somen noodles are vegan.

Udon noodles are thick white noodles made of wheat. They are most often served in hot soups, but they are also robust enough for stir-frying. When purchasing udon noodles, always go for the fresh noodles, which are either frozen or vacuum sealed. Some brands sell dried straight noodles, which they also call "udon" noodles, but these are not the real deal and will give you a very different finish. Udon noodles are vegan.

Wheat noodles are made of wheat flour and water (similar to the homemade hand-pulled noodles on page 76), and have a sturdy texture and consistency. They are sold either fresh or dried. Wheat noodles have a springy texture and are a good "any occasion" noodle that can be adapted to most dishes, particularly stir-fries or soups. Wheat noodles are vegan.

Easy homemade hand-pulled noodles

On any given day, dried noodles or store-bought fresh noodles are my go-to. But every now and then it's fun to make my own, just to prove I can. The first time I attempted homemade noodles, my mother happened to call on FaceTime, right as I was rolling the dough. She stayed on the line and, from the other side of the world, watched me struggle with the unwieldy strands of dough. She told me homemade noodles were "really hard to make," perhaps hinting that I was bound for failure or maybe that I shouldn't try at all. Like the dutiful daughter that I have always been, I rolled my eyes and kept going. I live for these snarky yet light-hearted exchanges with my mother. Her criticism is actually encouragement in disguise; it makes me smile. As my mother suspected, my first batch of homemade noodles was not perfect, but they weren't awful either, and the process was so easy that I now make them regularly.

So now I'm encouraging *you* to try making them, just to prove you can! The dough is made with just three basic ingredients—flour, salt and water. With just a bit of elbow grease and patience, you will have a batch of chewy, toothsome noodles, which are intensely satisfying to the bite. I make my dough by hand, but you could definitely use the dough hook on a stand mixer to knead the dough—if you choose to do this, you may still need to knead it by hand to ensure it's nice and smooth. I usually cut my noodles into wide ribbons—it makes them easier to handle and I like the way they grip onto the sauce.

SERVES 4

3 cups (450 g) bread flour or all-purpose flour, plus extra for dusting

2 teaspoons sea salt

Make the dough

Combine the flour and salt in a large bowl. Using a pair of chopsticks, gradually stir in ¾ cup plus 2 tablespoons (225 ml) of room-temperature water, a little at a time. It will look dry and rough—this is normal. Using your hands, bring the dough together, incorporating any dry bits of flour. When the dough comes together into a large ball, turn it out onto a smooth work surface (preferably not wood) and knead for 8–10 minutes, until the dough is smooth and malleable. Cover in plastic wrap and allow to rest at room temperature for 45 minutes. You can also leave it to rest overnight in the fridge—just make sure you bring it back to room temperature before the next step.

Roll out the dough

After the first resting period, knead the dough for 2–3 minutes, then rest it again for 15–20 minutes—this relaxes the gluten and makes the dough easier to roll out. By now, the surface will look very smooth. Sprinkle your work surface with a little flour and divide the dough into four equal pieces. Working with one piece at a time (keep the others covered with a damp tea towel), roll it out into a roughly 9 x 12-inch (22.5 x 30 cm) rectangle (dust the rolling pin or surface with more flour if the dough sticks). If at any time the dough bounces back too much when you are rolling, simply leave it to relax for a few minutes. The more time you let it rest, the easier it will be to work with.

Cut and pull the dough

Lightly dust the dough with flour and, using a sharp knife, cut it into
½-inch-wide (1.25 cm) strips. Lift up each strip and gently pull, running
your thumb and index finger along the noodle to elongate the strand.
You don't have to pull too hard, just enough to slightly stretch the
dough. Dust the strands with more flour to stop them sticking. Transfer
the noodles to a floured sheet pan, cover with a tea towel, and repeat
with the remaining dough.

Cook the noodles

Bring a large saucepan of well-salted water to the boil. Add the noodles
in batches of two or three handfuls (depending on the size of your pan)
and cook for 2–3 minutes, until the noodles float to the surface. Remove
them from the water with tongs. Fresh noodles stick together easily so
dress them immediately with a few drops of sesame or vegetable oil.
If you plan on eating them later, submerge the noodles in an ice bath;
when ready to serve, reheat them in boiling water for about 1 minute.

Fresh noodles can be used to make noodle soups, fried noodles or
salads. I particularly enjoy these noodles with lashings of everything
oil (see page 25), peanut butter sauce (see page 85) or with tomato and
egg (see page 79).

Note: You can also freeze these noodles. Dust them with rice flour to
separate the strands and place them on a parchment paper–lined sheet,
then place the tray in the freezer. Once frozen, transfer the noodles to
a freezer container or bag. To cook, plunge the frozen noodles straight
into boiling water (do not thaw first) and cook until they float to the top.

Tomato and egg rice noodles

SERVES 4
GLUTEN FREE

Ice cubes

6 beefsteak tomatoes (about 2 pounds / 900 g)

6 large eggs, lightly beaten

Vegetable or other neutral oil

1-inch (2.5 cm) piece of ginger, peeled and finely chopped

1 small onion, cut into thin wedges

3 tablespoons brown sugar

10½ ounces (300 g) thick rice noodles (fresh or dried)

3 scallions, finely sliced

Sea salt and white pepper

Everything Oil (see page 25), to serve

"Tomato and egg" is a comforting dish, more often eaten at home than at restaurants. Growing up, this tomato and egg dish was fairly nondescript, a blip on my mother's roster of big-flavored Cantonese dishes. My mum's version is sweet and syrupy, and memorable too, mainly because she rarely cooked or served tomatoes. But after I moved to America, this dish took on a new significance. It became an antidote for my homesickness, and fed my nostalgia for home cooking. I have since found this dish in a few tucked-away restaurants in New York City, but it's also super easy to make at home. Tomato and egg is usually eaten with copious amounts of white rice, but here I've teamed it with rice noodles to warm the heart and soul.

Set up a large bowl with ice and cold water—this is your ice bath for peeling the tomatoes. Bring a saucepan of water to the boil. Score a small "x" at the bottom of each tomato and add them to the boiling water until the skins wrinkle and split—this should take 1-1½ minutes. Remove from the water and drop them straight into the ice bath. Once the tomatoes are cool, lift them out of the water and peel away their skin. Chop the tomato flesh.

Lightly season the beaten egg with a little sea salt and a small pinch of white pepper.

Heat a wok or large frying pan over high heat. When hot, add 1–2 tablespoons of vegetable oil and pour in the egg. Leave it for about 20–30 seconds so it sets slightly on the bottom, then turn off the heat and move the egg around the wok or pan to scramble (it will finish cooking in the residual heat). When the egg is just firm, remove it from the wok or pan and set aside.

Heat another 1–2 tablespoons of vegetable oil in the same wok or pan, add the ginger and onion and fry over high heat for 30 seconds. Add the tomato and stir well, then cover and cook over medium–low heat for 5 minutes. Add the brown sugar and a splash of water, and squash the tomato a little to break it up. Reduce the heat to low, then cover and cook for another 2 minutes. Return the egg to the wok or pan, season well with sea salt and white pepper and gently toss to combine.

Meanwhile, bring a large saucepan of salted water to the boil, add the rice noodles and cook according to the packet instructions until just soft, about 6–7 minutes. Drain and immediately place the noodles in four bowls. Top with the tomato and egg stir-fry and scatter with the scallions. I like to drizzle lots of everything oil over the top just before serving.

Cacio e pepe udon noodles

SERVES 4

28 ounces (800 g) udon noodles

6 tablespoons (85 g) salted butter, cubed

1 tablespoon freshly ground black pepper, plus extra to serve

2 tablespoons white (shiro) miso

2 ounces (60 g) pecorino, finely grated

Sea salt

The idea for this dish came to me while I was in Japan, where hybrid cooking is executed with unparalleled flair and precision. At Shin Udon, a sliver of a restaurant in Tokyo's Shibuya, they serve not only the best udon dish I've ever eaten (see page 89 for my life-changing udon recipe inspired by this experience), but they also offer a carbonara-inspired noodle dish that comes topped with butter, pepper, Parmesan and bacon tempura. My son ordered this dish and it was as decadent as it sounds. Inspired by this melting pot of flavors, this recipe pairs another Italian classic, pecorino and black pepper, with burly udon noodles. The little hint of miso adds an extra layer of deliciousness. This dish is destined to become a family staple.

Bring a saucepan of salted water to the boil. Add the noodles and blanch them for about 30 seconds, stirring with chopsticks to separate the strands. Drain immediately, reserving about 1 cup (250 ml) of the cooking water.

Melt 4 tablespoons (60 g) of the butter in a large frying pan over medium heat. Add the black pepper and stir for 20–30 seconds, until fragrant and toasted. Pour in about half the reserved cooking water, then add the noodles, miso and remaining butter. Turn off the heat, then add half the pecorino and season with a little sea salt. Toss the noodles until the cheese melts and the noodles are well coated (if the noodles seem dry, add some more of the reserved cooking water).

Transfer to serving plates and top with the remaining pecorino and, if you like, more pepper.

Substitute

Udon: rice noodles or ramen noodles

Pecorino: Parmesan

Veganize

Use vegan butter and nutritional yeast instead of pecorino

Shawarma "Singapore" noodles with corn and cauliflower

SERVES 4–6
VEGAN AND GLUTEN FREE

Vegetable or other neutral oil
1 onion, finely sliced
1 small (about 1⅓ pounds / 600 g) cauliflower, cut into florets
1 garlic clove, grated
7 ounces (200 g) corn kernels (from 2 corn cobs)
10½ ounces (300 g) rice vermicelli, soaked in warm water for 5–10 minutes
1 cup (155 g) fresh or frozen peas
2 scallions, finely sliced
Sea salt and white pepper
Maggi Seasoning Sauce, to serve (optional)

Shawarma spice

1 tablespoon ground cumin
2 teaspoons ground coriander
2 teaspoons smoked paprika
2 teaspoons sea salt
Black pepper

This dish is a riff on Singapore-style curry noodles. Our whole family adores Singapore noodles, especially my mother's version—when my son Huck was a baby, he loved them so much she made them for his first birthday party. This particular recipe is a bit of a happy accident—it came about one day when I was making Singapore noodles and I spotted a bottle of New York Shuk's shawarma spice on the condiment tray next to my wok. I unscrewed the lid and took a whiff—I loved the smell so much, I instantly decided to use the shawarma instead of the curry powder. The result was spectacular, and suddenly, shawarma noodles became a thing! Of course, if you want to make traditional Singapore noodles, simply substitute the shawarma spice with a mild curry powder (see page 18).

To make the shawarma spice, combine all the ingredients in a small jar and shake well.

Heat a wok or large frying pan over high heat. When hot, add 1 tablespoon of oil, then the onion and cook, stirring often, for 2 minutes until fragrant. Add the cauliflower, season with sea salt and stir-fry for 3–4 minutes until just tender. Add the garlic and corn and toss for another minute. Remove from the wok or pan and set aside.

Drain the vermicelli. Return the wok or pan to medium heat, add about 2 tablespoons of oil and the shawarma spice and cook for 15–20 seconds, stirring constantly to prevent burning. Add the vermicelli, along with a bit more oil, and toss until the noodles are heated through and thoroughly coated in the spice mix. Return the cauliflower mixture to the pan, along with the peas, 2–3 big pinches of sea salt and a pinch of white pepper, and toss until everything is well mixed and the peas are cooked, about 1–2 minutes.

Remove from the heat and add the scallions. Taste and season with sea salt and white pepper. Sprinkle over a few drops of Maggi, if you like, and serve.

Cold peanut butter green tea noodles with cucumber

Originally a Sichuan dish, cold peanut butter or sesame noodles have become an American take-out classic. There are many variations of this dish—for cold sesame noodles, simply use sesame paste or tahini in place of the peanut butter (see my recipe on page 87), or make "mala noodles" by adding an enthusiastic lashing of tongue-numbing chile oil (very similar to my everything oil on page 25). The crucial step for this dish is to mix the peanut butter sauce with the chilled noodles right before you are ready to eat—if the noodles sit in the sauce too long, they will become soggy. These noodles are served cold; cooling them in an ice bath ensures that they stay firm and sturdy enough to handle the heavy peanut butter sauce.

While I have used earthy green tea noodles here, this sauce will go with any type of noodle. Try soba, ramen or rice noodles. Don't have noodles? Substitute a long pasta such as fettucine or linguine.

SERVES 4
VEGAN

3 Persian cucumbers, trimmed

Ice cubes

7 ounces (200 g) green tea noodles

½ cup (80 g) roasted peanuts, roughly chopped

2 scallions, finely sliced

Sea salt and black pepper

Everything Oil (see page 25) or chile oil, to serve (optional)

Peanut butter sauce

1 tablespoon toasted sesame oil

⅓ cup (90 g) smooth peanut butter

1 teaspoon maple syrup

½-inch (1.25 cm) piece of ginger, peeled and finely chopped

1 small garlic clove, finely chopped

2 teaspoons rice vinegar

Sea salt and black pepper

Cut the cucumbers in half lengthwise and, using a small spoon, scrape out the seeds. Slice the cucumber into very thin strips. Set aside.

Set up a large bowl with ice and cold water—this is your ice bath for the noodles. Bring a large saucepan of salted water to the boil, add the noodles and cook according to the packet instructions until tender, about 5–6 minutes. Drain and rinse under cold running water until the noodles are cold; drain and place in the ice bath. Set aside.

To make the peanut butter sauce, whisk together the sesame oil, peanut butter, maple syrup, ginger, garlic and vinegar. Thin the sauce with ⅓ cup (80 ml) of warm water (or more) until it has a pourable consistency. Season well with sea salt and black pepper. Set aside.

When you are ready to eat, drain the noodles, shaking off any excess water. Place the noodles in a large bowl, then pour over the peanut butter sauce and toss to coat the noodles. Add half the cucumber and half the peanuts, then season well with sea salt and black pepper. Toss to combine.

To serve, scatter the remaining cucumber, peanuts and scallions over the noodles. Top with a few drops of everything oil, or chile oil if you like it hot, and eat immediately.

Substitute

Peanut butter: tahini

Green tea noodles: soba, rice, egg, udon or ramen noodles, or long pasta

Sesame rice noodles with "everything oil" and charred broccoli

SERVES 4
VEGAN AND GLUTEN FREE

Tahini may not seem like an obvious sauce for noodles, but it is not as unusual as it sounds. Sesame noodles is a popular Sichuan dish, traditionally made with Chinese sesame paste and usually served cold. The Chinese version of sesame paste is similar to tahini, but is made with sesame seeds that are deeply toasted before grinding, resulting in a deep brown paste that is slightly thicker, with a consistency akin to peanut butter. Since tahini is much more accessible and a pantry staple, it is my preferred ingredient for this quick weeknight dish. I like my sesame noodles with a hefty amount of heat, and the complex flavors of my everything oil work perfectly here. Make this dish your own by adding whatever roasted vegetables you have on hand.

10½ ounces (300 g) dried thick rice noodles

2 teaspoons toasted sesame oil

½ cup (135 g) tahini

1 garlic clove, grated

Extra-virgin olive oil

2 heads (about 1¾ pounds / 750 g) broccoli, cut into florets

2–3 tablespoons Everything Oil (see page 25)

2 scallions, finely sliced

Handful of cilantro leaves

Sea salt and black pepper

Bring a large saucepan of salted water to the boil and cook the rice noodles according to the packet instructions until al dente, about 6–7 minutes. Drain and rinse under cold water, then drain again. Add the sesame oil and toss to coat the noodles.

Whisk together the tahini, garlic and ½–¾ cup (125–185 ml) of room-temperature water until smooth, with a pourable consistency. Season with sea salt and black pepper.

Heat a large frying pan or grill pan over high heat. When hot, drizzle with olive oil, add the broccoli florets and season with sea salt and black pepper. Cook, turning regularly, for 5–7 minutes until charred and just tender.

In a large bowl, combine the noodles, charred broccoli and tahini sauce, and drizzle with olive oil. Season with sea salt and black pepper. Transfer the noodles to individual bowls and drizzle with as much (or as little) everything oil as you like. Top with scallions and cilantro. Eat at room temperature.

Substitute

Rice noodles: ramen, udon or egg noodles

Everything Oil: chile oil, Rayu (see page 26) or chile flakes

Broccoli: kale, cauliflower or Brussels sprouts

Tahini: peanut butter

Life-changing udon with soft-boiled egg, hot soy and black pepper

In a diminutive noodle shop called Shin Udon, a short walk from Shinjuku station in Tokyo, I savored a bowl of udon noodles that would ruin me for all other noodle experiences. Perhaps it's unfair to compare all noodles to this—the thick, chewy strands are made fresh, moments before they are served (we spent half an hour watching the noodle maker at work while we waited for a table). My bowl of udon with hot soy, soft-boiled egg, butter and black pepper blew my mind and entranced my taste buds. As I slurped the toothsome, salty strands, I knew I was having a life-changing experience.

While there is no way to truly replicate this unforgettable experience at home, my humble rendition of Shin Udon's incomparable noodle dish is still satisfying and crave-worthy.

SERVES 4

4 large eggs

28 ounces (800 g) udon noodles

2 cups (500 ml) vegetable stock

¼ cup (60 ml) tamari or soy sauce

2 teaspoons mirin

6 tablespoons (85 g) salted butter, cubed

4 scallions, finely sliced

1 tablespoon toasted sesame oil

Sea salt and black pepper

Bring a small saucepan of water to the boil. Add the eggs and set the timer for 6 minutes. As soon as the buzzer goes, immediately drain the eggs into a colander and place under cold running water until they are completely cold. (This will make very soft-boiled eggs—if you prefer a firmer yolk, cook them for another minute.) Peel and set aside.

Cook the udon noodles in a large saucepan of salted water according to the packet instructions until al dente. This will take 1–3 minutes, depending on whether your noodles are fresh, vacuum-sealed or frozen. Drain, then scoop the hot noodles into four bowls.

Meanwhile, combine the stock, tamari or soy sauce and mirin in a small saucepan and place over low heat until hot.

Pour the hot soy sauce over each bowl of noodles and top with a soft-boiled egg. Add a knob of butter and allow it to melt into the noodles. Add the scallions and scatter a generous amount of black pepper over the noodles (use as much pepper as you like, but this dish is intended to be very peppery). Finish with a little drizzle of sesame oil and sprinkle with sea salt.

Veganize

Omit the eggs and use vegan butter

Buttery miso Vegemite noodles

There are some recipes that I have carried around in my head for years. This is one of them. It's not your everyday noodle dish, but once you have tasted it, you will likely want to eat it often. The noodles feature umami to the highest degree, with an unlikely combination of Vegemite, miso paste and butter creating an impossibly addictive noodle dish.

Like many Australians, I have a deep affection for Vegemite. As a kid, a Vegemite sandwich (made by my mum with not quite the right ratio of Vegemite to margarine) represented assimilation and acceptance. I felt infinitely more Australian as I chowed down on a squashed Vegemite sandwich on the playground. While Vegemite is virtually the national dish of Australia, people around the world have a love/hate (mostly hate in my experience) relationship with the rich, yeasty sandwich spread. This recipe might be the one that finally convinces doubters, but if you're not a convert, just omit the Vegemite and double the amount of miso.

Bring a large saucepan of salted water to the boil and cook the noodles according to the packet instructions until al dente, about 2–4 minutes. Drain, reserving about ½ cup (125 ml) of the cooking water, and refresh the noodles under cold running water. Drain again.

Add the butter to the same pan and swirl it around, allowing it to melt over medium heat. Remove from the heat and whisk in the Vegemite and miso paste until smooth and well combined. Drop in the noodles and, using tongs or chopsticks, toss to coat in the miso and Vegemite sauce. If the noodles look or feel dry, add a touch of oil or some of the reserved cooking water.

Transfer to serving bowls and season with black pepper. Sprinkle over the grated cheese and chives and serve.

SERVES 4

12 ounces (350 g) instant dried ramen or egg noodles

6 tablespoons (85 g) unsalted butter

1½ tablespoons Vegemite

1½ tablespoons white (shiro) miso paste

Extra-virgin olive oil (optional)

Black pepper

½ cup (60 g) grated cheddar cheese

Handful of chopped chives

Substitute

Vegemite: Marmite or Promite

Chives: scallions

Veganize

Use vegan butter and replace the cheddar with nutritional yeast or non-dairy cheese

Celery, mushroom and leek "dan dan" noodles

Spicy, nutty, salty, with a slight acidity, dan dan noodles are full of personality, and very different from the comparatively mellow chow meins and ho funs of my childhood. Dan dan noodles come from northern China, a region known for its bold flavors and spiciness. I first came across this dish in New York, at one of the many no-name noodle houses in Chinatown; I had never eaten this type of cuisine as a child, so discovering these flavors felt exciting. A street food in Sichuan, the dish is named after the type of pole (dan dan) used by vendors to carry baskets of noodles and sauce across their shoulders. Traditionally, dan dan noodles are made with pork and a fermented mustard pickle called sui mi ya cai (I've omitted this because it can be quite hard to find). My version is vegan, featuring mushrooms, celery and leek, which combine to impart an aromatic potency.

SERVES 4
VEGAN

1 pound (450 g) fresh wheat noodles

Vegetable or peanut oil

2 celery stalks, finely diced

1 leek, halved lengthwise and finely sliced

10½ ounces (300 g) cremini or button mushrooms, finely diced

1 garlic clove, finely chopped

1 tablespoon toasted white sesame seeds

Handful of cilantro leaves

2 scallions, finely sliced

Sea salt and white pepper

Everything Oil (see page 25) or chile oil, to serve

Dan dan sauce

1-inch (2.5 cm) piece of ginger, peeled and finely chopped

2 garlic cloves, finely chopped

2 tablespoons rice vinegar

2 tablespoons tamari or soy sauce

2 tablespoons Everything Oil (see page 25), chile oil or chile flakes (or to taste)

1 teaspoon toasted sesame oil

¼ cup (67 g) tahini

2 teaspoons sugar

For the dan dan sauce, whisk together all the ingredients with 1 tablespoon of water in a small bowl.

Bring a large saucepan of salted water to the boil. Add the noodles and cook according to the packet instructions until al dente, about 3–4 minutes. Drain and rinse under cold water.

In a wok or large frying pan set over medium–high heat, drizzle about 1 tablespoon of oil, then add the celery and leek and cook for 2–3 minutes until softened and fragrant. Add the mushrooms and garlic and cook for 4–5 minutes. The mushrooms will release a lot of juice as they cook—let it evaporate, then continue cooking until they turn golden and start to caramelize. Season with two big pinches of sea salt and a small pinch of white pepper and remove from the heat.

Add the noodles to the mushroom mixture and pour in the dan dan sauce. Toss to combine, making sure the noodles are well coated. Top with the sesame seeds, cilantro and scallions and drizzle with everything oil or chile oil.

Substitute

Fresh noodles: 10½ ounces (300 g) dried noodles, any variety

Tahini: peanut butter

Use rice noodles or glass noodles for gluten free

Sheet pan chow mein

Cantonese chow mein is well known for its contrasting textures—crispy fried strands tangled with soft noodles, tender-crisp veggies, all smothered in an umami-rich sauce. While the wok is still the traditional (and arguably the best) cooking vessel for chow mein, a humble sheet pan is also a handy way to rustle it up with minimal effort. Simply throw everything on a sheet pan and let the oven do the work for you. It's also a great way to use up leftover vegetables or seasonal produce. Dried (or fresh) thin egg noodles are generally best for chow mein, as they crisp up nicely, but if you're less concerned about crispiness, use whatever noodles you have on hand.

SERVES 4

1 bell pepper (any color), finely sliced

1 carrot, peeled and finely sliced diagonally

1 broccoli head, cut into florets

1 tablespoon toasted sesame oil

Extra-virgin olive oil

9 ounces (255 g) dried thin egg noodles

1 (8.8-ounce / 250-g) can cut baby corn, drained

5 ounces (140 g) asparagus, woody ends trimmed, cut into 2-inch (5 cm) pieces

1 scallion, finely sliced

Handful of cilantro leaves

2 tablespoons toasted white sesame seeds

Sea salt

Soy seasoning

1 tablespoon toasted sesame oil

¼ cup (60 ml) soy sauce, tamari or coconut aminos

1 tablespoon vegetarian stir-fry sauce

¼ teaspoon white pepper

1 small garlic clove, grated

Preheat the oven to 400°F (200°C).

Place the bell pepper, carrot and broccoli on a half sheet pan (about 13 x 18 inches / 32.5 x 45 cm), drizzle with the sesame oil and a splash of olive oil and season with sea salt. Toss to coat in the oil, then bake for 10 minutes until the vegetables are starting to soften.

Meanwhile, bring a large saucepan of salted water to the boil. Add the egg noodles, and cook according to the packet instructions until al dente, about 4–5 minutes. Drain and cool under cold running water. Drain well again and pat dry with a clean tea towel.

For the soy seasoning, combine all the ingredients in a small bowl.

Remove the sheet pan from the oven and push the vegetables to the side. Add the noodles, corn and asparagus. Drizzle the noodles with olive oil, season with sea salt and toss well to coat. Return the sheet pan to the oven and bake for 15–18 minutes, until the noodles are crispy on the top and bottom. You are looking for a combination of crispy and non-crispy noodles.

Remove the sheet pan from the oven, drizzle over the soy seasoning and toss well. Scatter over the scallion, cilantro and sesame seeds and serve.

Substitute

Broccoli: Asian greens

Asparagus: sugar snap peas or snow peas

Vegetarian stir-fry sauce: omit if unavailable

Egg noodles: ramen noodles

Veganize

Use wheat noodles

Spicy sesame "tantanmen" ramen

This recipe is inspired by the tantanmen noodles from T's TanTan, a modest vegan ramen shop hidden away in a Tokyo train station. This bowl of ramen happens to be vegan, but no matter what your dietary choices are, you will love it. My son Dash declared it his favorite ramen of all the ones we tried in Tokyo and Kyoto. Rich and spicy with complex flavors, the robust sesame-based broth is topped with crumbled soy meat and will leave you salivating for more.

My tantanmen is a creamy, spicy, sesame-laced soy milk ramen, topped with seasoned crumbled tofu. Serve the ramen in a timely fashion—leaving the noodles in hot broth for too long overcooks them and makes them soggy.

Bring a large saucepan of salted water to the boil, add the noodles and cook according to the packet instructions until al dente, about 4–5 minutes. About 30 seconds before they are ready, add the Asian greens and bean sprouts and blanch quickly. Drain and refresh under cold running water, then drain again.

For the seasoned tofu, place a large frying pan over medium heat, add the sesame oil, garlic and ginger and fry for 30–60 seconds until fragrant. Add the crumbled tofu, season with sea salt and fry over high heat for 2 minutes. Add the mirin, tamari or soy sauce and miso paste and cook, undisturbed, for another 2–3 minutes, until the tofu is crispy. Remove from the heat and set aside.

Prepare the soup base by whisking together the tahini, vinegar, tamari or soy sauce and rayu or chile oil until a chunky paste forms. Pour the stock and soy milk into a saucepan and heat over medium–low heat until hot, but not boiling. Turn off the heat and whisk in the tahini paste. Taste and season with sea salt if needed.

Place a handful of ramen noodles, greens and bean sprouts in each bowl and top with the seasoned tofu and corn. Ladle in the soup base, covering the noodles and vegetables. Top with sesame seeds, scallions and a few drops of rayu or chile oil and serve.

SERVES 4
VEGAN

10½ ounces (300 g) dried ramen noodles

9 ounces (255 g) Asian greens

9 ounces (255 g) bean sprouts

7 ounces (200 g) corn kernels (from 2 corn cobs)

2–3 tablespoons toasted white sesame seeds

4 scallions, finely sliced

Sea salt

Rayu (see page 26) or chile oil, to serve

Seasoned tofu

1 tablespoon toasted sesame oil

2 garlic cloves, finely chopped

1-inch (2.5 cm) piece of ginger, peeled and finely chopped

14 ounces (400 g) tofu, finely crumbled

1 tablespoon mirin

1 tablespoon tamari or soy sauce

1 tablespoon white (shiro) miso paste

Sea salt

Soup base

1 cup (270 g) tahini

1 tablespoon rice vinegar

⅓ cup (80 ml) tamari or soy sauce

2–4 teaspoons Rayu (see page 26) or chile oil

3 cups (750 ml) vegetable stock

4 cups (1 liter) unsweetened soy milk

Sea salt (optional)

Substitute

Dried ramen: 28 ounces (800 g) fresh ramen noodles

Fresh corn kernels: 1 cup (150 g) frozen corn kernels

Soy milk: coconut milk, oat milk or nut milk such as macadamia

Tahini: peanut or almond butter

Use mung bean vermicelli or rice noodles for gluten free

Sour and spiced coconut noodle soup

My mother rarely cooked with coconut milk. She said it was a "fatty" ingredient, but I suspect her dislike was more because she was unfamiliar with its sweet, tropical creaminess. But whenever she added a dash (and I mean the tiniest dash) to her potato curry it would disappear in a flash. I think this is the power of coconut milk— it brings the "extra," the special quality that makes a dish irresistible. This recipe is inspired by the rich aromatic intensity of tom kha gai, the coconut soup that you might order at your favorite Thai restaurant. I love the depth of this soup, which boasts kaleidoscopic layers of tanginess, saltiness, sourness and sweetness, while still feeling bright and light. This is the simplest of noodle soups, radiating with exciting flavors.

SERVES 4
VEGAN AND GLUTEN FREE

10½ ounces (300 g) rice noodles

1–2 long green or red chiles, finely sliced

Handful of cilantro leaves

2 scallions, finely chopped

Sea salt and black pepper

Thin slices of lime, to serve (optional)

Sour and spiced coconut broth

Vegetable oil

2 lemongrass stalks, white parts only, finely chopped

1 shallot, finely diced

1-inch (2.5 cm) piece of ginger (or galangal if you have it), finely chopped

1 (13.5-ounce / 398 ml) can coconut milk

4 cups (1 liter) vegetable stock

5–6 makrut lime leaves, torn and bruised (optional)

4 fresh shiitake, oyster or button mushrooms, finely sliced

1–2 small sweet potatoes (about 10½ ounces / 300 g), peeled and cut into small cubes

1 lime, halved

Sea salt and black pepper

Substitute

Green or red chiles: red chile flakes

Sweet potato: butternut squash

Rice noodles: ramen, somen or udon noodles

For the coconut broth, pour a drizzle of oil into a saucepan, add the lemongrass, shallot, ginger and a pinch of sea salt and cook over low heat for 1 minute or until aromatic. Add the coconut milk, stock, makrut lime leaves, mushrooms and sweet potato and season with sea salt and black pepper. Increase the heat to bring it to a gentle boil, then simmer over low heat for 8–10 minutes until the vegetables are cooked through. Turn off the heat and add some lime juice, to taste. Check the seasoning and add more sea salt, if required.

Meanwhile, bring a saucepan of salted water to the boil, add the rice noodles and cook according to the packet instructions until just al dente, about 6–7 minutes. Drain and divide the noodles among serving bowls.

Ladle the hot coconut broth over the noodles, then top with sliced chiles, cilantro leaves and scallions, and season with sea salt and black pepper. Squeeze over some more lime juice and add some sliced lime, if you like it more sour.

Red curry laksa noodle soup

Malaysian laksa noodle soup is a staple of food courts in Australia, but in other parts of the world it is much harder to find. Like many Australian expats, I crave laksa. When I go home, I will eat it every chance I get—at suburban shopping centers, at airports and most often at Sydney laksa institution "Jimmy's Recipe" (luckily Jimmy's is downstairs from Kinokuniya, one of my favorite bookshops). In Malaysia, each region boasts its own wondrous version of laksa—some are coconutty, others brim with tamarind, while some are heavy with belacan (shrimp paste). I have made my own laksa paste for years, but in this recipe I've cut a few corners by using a store-bought red curry or laksa paste (available from most supermarkets). While commercial curry pastes are generally not as flavorful as homemade ones—they do provide an excellent canvas for building a richly aromatic soup, quickly. Here, the addition of curry and lime leaves adds a luxurious depth of flavor. Both types of leaves freeze well so stick any extras straight in the freezer.

For the laksa soup, place a large saucepan over medium heat. Add the oil, garlic and ginger and stir for 30 seconds, until aromatic. Add the curry paste and continue stirring for another 30 seconds, then add the stock, coconut milk, curry leaves, makrut lime leaves, brown sugar and sea salt and bring to a gentle boil. Cover and cook over low heat for 8–10 minutes, until the flavors are cohesive.

Meanwhile, bring a large saucepan of salted water to the boil, add the noodles and cook according to the packet instructions (I usually cook both types of noodles together as fresh noodles and rice vermicelli have a similar cooking time, but check the times on your packet). When the noodles are al dente, drain, refresh in cold water and drain again.

Add the tofu cubes and greens to the laksa soup and cook for 1 minute, just until they are heated through. Taste and season with sea salt. Divide the two types of noodles among four bowls and pour over the laksa soup. Top with the bean sprouts, lime wedges and any of the garnishes you are using.

SERVES 4

9 ounces (255 g) fresh egg noodles, such as hokkien

9 ounces (255 g) rice vermicelli

9 ounces (255 g) firm tofu, cubed

7 ounces (200 g) Asian greens or broccoli

3½ ounces (100 g) bean sprouts

1–2 limes, cut into wedges

Sea salt

Laksa soup

1 tablespoon toasted sesame oil

1 large garlic clove, finely chopped

1-inch (2.5 cm) piece of ginger, peeled and finely chopped

2 tablespoons store-bought vegan red curry or laksa paste

4 cups (1 liter) vegetable stock

1 (13.5-ounce / 398 ml) can coconut milk

2 curry leaves (fresh or dried)

4 makrut lime leaves

2 tablespoons brown sugar

2 teaspoons sea salt

Garnishes (optional, but recommended)

Crispy fried scallions

Handful of cilantro leaves

Finely sliced red chile

Veganize

Omit the egg noodles and use more rice vermicelli, or add mung bean vermicelli for vegan and gluten free

Wontons and noodles in ginger–turmeric broth

SERVES 4
VEGAN

About 20 wontons (see page 123)

10½ ounces (300 g) somen or other thin wheat noodles

1 bunch (about 9 ounces / 255 g) of broccolini, trimmed and stalks halved

1 scallion, finely sliced

Handful of cilantro leaves

1 serrano or long green chile, finely sliced (optional)

Ginger–turmeric broth

2 ounces (60 g) ginger, peeled

Extra-virgin olive oil

2 garlic cloves, finely chopped

1 teaspoon ground turmeric

6 cups (1.5 liters) vegetable stock

1 (14-ounce / 400-g) can chickpeas, drained

Sea salt and black pepper

Substitute

Somen noodles: udon, soba or rice noodles

Broccolini: broccoli, baby bok choy, Chinese broccoli or kale

Canned chickpeas: 9 ounces (255 g) soaked, cooked chickpeas

Use rice noodles for gluten free

In Chinese culture, soup is medicine, a revered elixir to address both everyday ailments and serious illness. When we were kids (and even now), any tingle of a cold or sniffle sent my mother straight to her "medicine pantry" to select the right blend of dried herbal ingredients to brew a restorative tong (soup). Most of these Chinese herbs were foreign to me—some looked like thin white bark, or dehydrated sticks. Others I now recognize as dried longan (a fleshy fruit similar to lychee), dried jujube dates, lotus seeds and goji berries. As kids, we scoffed at my mum's attempts at homemade medicine, skeptical of her efforts to heal through food. The turning point for me was when I discovered the medicinal power of ginger. My mother's ginger fried rice would become my ultimate hangover cure, and an important postpartum food—while I was recovering from childbirth, my mother would bring me thermos flasks filled with ginger fried rice, to help my body heal. Nowadays, ginger is my everything ingredient, the one that makes me feel better when I feel poorly, and the flavor that stirs the warm embrace of nostalgia. This is a bowl of hearty comfort: wontons and noodles bathed in a ginger-spiced golden broth.

For the broth, halve the piece of ginger. Finely chop half of it and finely slice the rest. Add a splash of olive oil to a saucepan over medium heat and add the finely chopped ginger. Reduce the heat to low and stir for 1 minute. Add the garlic and turmeric and cook for another minute, stirring constantly to prevent burning. Add the stock, chickpeas and sliced ginger, then cover and simmer gently for 10 minutes. Taste and season with sea salt and black pepper.

Meanwhile, bring a large saucepan of salted water to the boil. Working in batches, add about six to eight wontons at a time; when they float to the top, cook for another 20 seconds, until the skin is translucent, then remove with a slotted spoon. Divide among four deep soup bowls.

In the same pan (top up with more water if you need to and bring to the boil again), add the noodles and cook according to the packet instructions until al dente, about 2 minutes. Drain, then place the noodles directly into the bowls with the wontons.

Just before you are ready to serve, add the broccolini to the broth and let it cook for 1–2 minutes, until just tender. Ladle the broth and broccolini over the noodles and wontons, and top with the scallion, cilantro and chile, if using.

Cold noodle soup with watermelon, kimchi and nashi pear

SERVES 4
VEGAN

9 ounces (255 g) somen or soba noodles

Ice cubes

1 cup (200 g) vegan kimchi or pickled vegetables

1 pound (450 g) watermelon, finely sliced and cut into triangles

1 nashi or Bosc pear, peeled, cored and sliced razor thin

2 Persian cucumbers, finely sliced into discs

2 jammy eggs (see page 33), halved

2 scallions, finely sliced

Cold vinegar broth

5 cups (1.25 liters) vegetable stock

2 tablespoons rice vinegar

2 tablespoons white vinegar

2 garlic cloves, smashed

1-inch (2.5 cm) piece of ginger, peeled and sliced

1 tablespoon sugar

Sea salt

Substitute

Watermelon: rockmelon, honeydew, daikon or radish

Nashi/pear: apple

Use cellophane, glass or mung bean noodles for gluten free

My mother always subscribed to the Chinese (and many other Asian cultures') mantra that eating hot or spicy food on hot days helps our body achieve balance, raising our internal temperature to match the temperature around us, increasing our blood circulation and making us sweat it out until we have ultimately cooled off. With this in mind, on a hot, steamy summer's day in New York City, we visited our favorite Korean restaurant, BCD Tofu House, for a bowl of soontofu, a spicy Korean tofu stew. While my children and I ordered our usual stews, my husband unexpectedly veered off course. He ordered a dish completely foreign to me—it was called naengmyeon. The noodles were in a clear vinegary broth dotted with ice cubes, with strips of nashi pear and daikon. With sweat beads on our brows, we all looked longingly at his ice-cold dish. Inspired by this icy goodness, my chilled soup is vinegary and sweet, with a hit of spice from the kimchi. The watermelon is an unusual addition, but it really works harmoniously with the cold broth.

For the broth, combine all the ingredients in a saucepan and place over medium heat. Bring to the boil, then reduce the heat and simmer for 10–15 minutes. Strain and season with more sea salt if needed, then set aside to cool. Refrigerate for at least an hour until completely cold.

Bring a large saucepan of salted water to the boil, add the noodles and cook according to the packet instructions until al dente, about 2–3 minutes. Drain and refresh under cold running water (or in an ice bath) until completely cold. Drain again.

Divide the noodles among bowls. Pour the broth evenly over the noodles and add a few ice cubes to the bowls. Top each serving with a mound of kimchi or pickled vegetables, watermelon, pear, cucumber and half an egg. Scatter with scallions and serve.

Note: The broth can be made ahead and kept in the fridge for up to 3 days.

Dumplings and other small thi gs

The master and her apprentice

It is not unusual for the kitchen to be the hub of a home, but for my mother, who came to Australia as a young woman looking for a new life, her cluttered suburban kitchen in Sydney became the place where she could keep her family traditions alive. With only her memory as a guide, she cooked myriad traditional and complex Cantonese dishes, many of which were long abandoned by her family and friends when they immigrated to Australia. Heirloom dishes like joong, a hefty bundle of salted glutinous rice stuffed with cured pork belly, salty-sweet lap cheong (Chinese sausage), dried baby shrimp and salted duck eggs became her signature. Her other coveted dish was gok jai dumplings.

Gok jai are traditional Cantonese-style dumplings with a distinctive transparent skin. Formed in a half-moon shape to resemble an ancient form of Chinese currency, gok jai are traditionally eaten around the New Year and for birthday or cultural celebrations, to bring good fortune. Growing up, I revered my mother's gok jai prowess; I would stand by and watch her deftly crimp one after another, until she had several trays filled with perfectly plump dumplings. I studied the way her nimble thumbs would effortlessly pleat the elegant braided edge, and longed to have my chance. My mother didn't often welcome kitchen helpers, but one day she finally relented and offered me a chair at her pull-out kitchen table, where she and I shared cooking duties for the first time. She cut off tiny balls of dough and handed them to me to flatten into thin discs. My mother watched over my crimping, eyes narrowed, silently critiquing. Every now and then, she would nod and tell me my crimping was "not bad," and I would beam like I'd just been paid the greatest compliment. With each dumpling, I felt like I was becoming more worthy of being my mother's daughter.

I have never forgotten my early apprenticeship as a dumpling assistant. Today, making dumplings is a form of meditation, a way for me to slow down and find balance in my daily life. As I fold and crimp, I am transported back to my childhood kitchen, working contentedly alongside my mother. Dumplings are my ultimate comfort food, and making them fills me with a sentimental yearning for that indescribable feeling of home, safety and fearlessness.

Dumpling wrappers

Making homemade dumpling wrappers from scratch may seem daunting, but they truly could not be easier. Just two humble ingredients—flour and water. The rest is up to alchemy (and a little bit of elbow grease, but not too much!).

This hot-water dough is one of my favorite things to make. It's such fun to work with because it's incredibly malleable and adaptable. The near-boiling water is the magic ingredient—the heat basically cooks the proteins in the flour, preventing the gluten from forming too much (reducing elasticity). This amounts to a robust dough that is extremely easy to roll out.

You can basically work with any temperature water: dough made with cold water tends to bounce back more so it's harder to roll, while warm water (about 125°F / 50°C) gives you a dough that is easier to work with, particularly if you plan on making and cooking the dumplings straight away. (If you put warm-water dough in the fridge, you will need to bring it back to room temperature before rolling out.) Most often, I opt for just-boiled water, which gives me a very malleable dough with almost no elasticity and that means that even if I have to pop it in the fridge, it comes out soft enough to roll.

MAKES ABOUT 24 WRAPPERS
VEGAN

2 cups (300 g) all-purpose flour, plus extra for dusting

¾ cup (185 ml) just-boiled water, cooled for about 2 minutes

Set a heatproof bowl on a tea towel (to stop it from moving around). Add the flour and make a well in the center. Using a wooden spoon or chopsticks, stir the flour as you slowly add the hot water in a steady stream. Try to moisten the flour as evenly as possible. Once the water has been added, it will look really shaggy. Taking care as it will be very hot, carefully knead the dough in the bowl to bring all the lumps together into one mass—if the dough is very dry and will not come together, you can add more warm water, one teaspoon at a time, until it is more workable.

Transfer the dough to a very lightly floured work surface. Knead the dough (by now it won't be hot) with the heel of your hand for about 2–3 minutes until smooth and elastic. Wrap the dough tightly in plastic wrap or place in a resealable plastic bag and allow to rest at room temperature for at least 30 minutes and up to 2 hours. During this time the dough will steam and become softer and easier to work with.

The dough is now ready to use, or you can refrigerate it overnight (you can roll it out while it is still cold).

Cut the dough into four even pieces. Working with one piece at a time (keep the others covered with a damp tea towel), roll it into a log shape. Cut the log into six pieces. Press each piece of dough into a disc and use a thin dowel or small rolling pin to roll each disc into a 4-inch (10-cm) round. The correct technique may take some time to master, but the basic principle is to make the edges of the dough a bit thinner than the center. Flour generously and set aside, covered with a tea towel. Continue with the remaining dough to make about 24 wrappers.

Another, perhaps easier, technique is to roll the dough into a flat sheet, like pie pastry, then cut out discs with a biscuit cutter. Lightly dust your work surface and rolling pin with flour and roll out the dough as thinly as you can, about $\frac{1}{16}$ inch (2 mm) is ideal. Use a well-floured 4-inch (10-cm) round biscuit cutter to cut out circles. Flour them well and cover with a tea towel. Re-roll the scraps and continue cutting until you have used all the dough. If the dough becomes resistant to rolling, cover it and let it rest until it softens again. This technique should give you 24–30 wrappers, depending on how thinly you roll the dough.

Hot-water dumpling dough is best for pan-fried and steamed dumplings.

Notes: You can also use a stand mixer to make this dough. Add the flour and water to the bowl and, using your dough hook attachment, mix on low speed until the water is incorporated. Increase the speed to medium and continue mixing for 2 minutes, until a dough forms. Transfer the dough to a lightly floured surface and knead for 1 minute, or until a ball forms. Wrap it in plastic wrap or a resealable plastic bag and rest for at least 30 minutes and up to 2 hours.

I don't recommend refrigerating these dumpling wrappers, but freezing is okay. Generously dust both sides of the wrappers with potato starch, tapioca or cornstarch. Stack the wrappers, wrap them in plastic and place in a resealable plastic bag or airtight container to freeze. Let the wrappers thaw on your counter and then use them as usual. The layer of starch means you will need to use water to seal the dumplings.

Gluten-free dumpling wrappers

**MAKES 28 WRAPPERS
VEGAN AND GLUTEN FREE**

¾ cup (100 g) tapioca flour

¾ cup (100 g) millet flour

1 cup (125 g) glutinous rice flour, plus extra for dusting

2 teaspoons psyllium husk

¾ cup (185 ml) just-boiled water, cooled for about 2 minutes

Vegetable or other neutral oil

While no one in my family has a gluten intolerance, it's always nice to switch things up—I often look for gluten-free alternatives in soy sauces, pastas and breads to give my body a break from gluten overload. This gluten-free dumpling dough is an excellent recipe to have up your sleeve—it is super simple to put together and produces hearty dumplings that are toothsome and satisfying. The dough is soft and lacks elasticity, so it's very easy to roll out. Pleating can be challenging with such a soft dough so I suggest either leaving the edge plain, or carefully crimping by curling the edges in, a tiny section at a time.

Combine all the dry ingredients in a bowl. Slowly stir in the just-boiled water, followed by 2 tablespoons of room-temperature water. Mix until combined, then knead it a little in the bowl until it comes together in a ball.

Flour your work surface with a little glutinous rice flour. Cut the dough into four even pieces. Working with one piece at a time (keep the others covered with a damp tea towel), roll it into a log shape, then cut each log into seven pieces.

To shape, roll each piece into a ball, then use a thin dowel or small rolling pin to roll each ball into a thin 4-inch (10 cm) disc. Place about 2 teaspoons of filling (see pages 118–119 for filling ideas) in the center and fold over into a half-moon shape. Press the edge together to enclose the filling and crimp, if you like.

Heat a large nonstick frying pan until hot, then add enough oil to lightly cover the base. Working in batches, add the dumplings and cook over medium–high heat until the bottom of the dumplings are lightly browned. Immediately add about ⅓ cup (80 ml) of water to the pan, just enough to cover the bottom of the dumplings, then cover and cook for 3–4 minutes, until the water has evaporated. Transfer the cooked dumplings to a plate and serve with your favorite dipping sauce.

Notes: This dough is best for pan-frying, but you can also steam or boil it on a gentle heat.

You could also replace this flour mix with a store-bought gluten-free flour mix. To do this, very slowly combine 2½ cups (285 g) of pre-mixed gluten-free flour with ¾ cup (185 ml) just-boiled water, mixing the water in slowly to evenly hydrate the flour (you don't need psyllium husk here as gluten-free mixes will already have a binding agent). Use as above. This makes about 30–32 dumplings.

Psyllium husk is available from health-food stores. If you can't find it, you could use ½ teaspoon of xanthan gum.

Remember, gluten-free dough has no elasticity, so don't overfill your dumpling as you won't be able to pull the dough over the filling like you can with regular dumpling dough. Handle the dough with care. If it cracks, you can re-roll it.

Dumplings, by the season

Making dumplings is one of my favorite things to do. It's my meditation, a quiet moment to enjoy the repetition of folding and crimping. At home, I like to experiment with dumpling fillings, trying different vegetables and flavors that are not particularly Asian. Leftovers can be easily repurposed into a dumpling filling—day-old beans or roasted veggies combined with spices or herbs make surprisingly tasty dumplings.

For me, dumplings are a wonderful blank canvas for both classic and new flavor pairings. This is my season-by-season tribute to nature's finest produce, all wrapped up in dumpling form. Some might say that these are "salad dumplings."

Tips for dumpling making

- Season your filling well. If it tastes bland before you stuff it into the wrapper, it will be even more tasteless as a dumpling, as the wrappers have no flavor.

- Make sure your filling is not too wet, as excessive moisture will break the dumpling wrapper. Remove as much liquid from vegetables as possible before adding to the mix (for greens, squeeze them tightly with your hands). If there is a pool of liquid, I recommend draining the entire mixture in a colander.

- If the mixture is too wet, you could also add some cornstarch or breadcrumbs to soak up the liquid.

- Don't overfill the dumplings. If you are new to making dumplings, less is more, and will give you more control over your crimping; once you become more comfortable with the process, you will be able to handle more filling.

- Store-bought dumpling wrappers are the best option for everyday cooking. I keep packets of round dumpling wrappers in my freezer and put them in the fridge to thaw overnight.

Each of the recipes on pages 118–119 makes enough filling for 15–20 dumplings, depending on the size of your wrappers and how much filling you use in each dumpling.

How to fold

If you are using store-bought dumpling wrappers, have a small bowl of water on hand—dip the very edge of the wrapper into the water and rotate it to wet the edge all the way around. If you are using homemade wrappers, there is no need to wet the edge. Hold the wrapper in the palm of your hand and place a spoonful of the filling in the center. Fold it over to form a semi-circle and pleat the edge from one corner to the other. Transfer to a sheet pan, "sitting" them so they are upright with a flat bottom. Cover the dumplings with a damp tea towel to keep them from drying out, and repeat with the remaining wrappers and filling.

How to cook

Pan-fried (potstickers): Heat a large frying pan over medium–high heat and, when hot, drizzle with vegetable oil. Working in batches, add the dumplings, flat-side down, and cook until the bottoms of the dumplings are lightly browned—this should take 1–2 minutes. Immediately add about 3 tablespoons of water to the pan, just enough to cover the base of the dumplings, then cover and cook for 3–4 minutes, or until the water has evaporated. Transfer the cooked dumplings to a plate and serve.

Steamed: Place the dumplings in a steamer that has been lined with parchment paper or napa (Chinese) cabbage leaves. Bring a saucepan of water to the boil, place the steamer over the boiling water, then cover and steam for 10–15 minutes.

Spring

Asparagus, mint and feta

Remove the woody ends from **12 ounces (350 g) of asparagus spears** and blanch them in boiling salted water for 1–2 minutes, until just tender-crisp and bright green. Drain and refresh under cold running water, then drain again. Finely chop the asparagus and combine with a **big handful of chopped mint leaves, 1 finely chopped garlic clove** and **3½ ounces (100 g) of crumbled feta**, stirring well to mash everything together. Season with **sea salt** and **black pepper**.

Peas and chives

Blanch **2 cups (310 g) of frozen or fresh peas** and add them to a blender, along with **1 finely chopped garlic clove**, and whiz to a chunky mash. Mix with **2 tablespoons of finely chopped chives** and season well with **sea salt** and **black pepper**. Add some **fresh ricotta** for a creamier dumpling, if you like.

Zucchini, pesto and goat's cheese

Grate **2 zucchini (about 1 pound / 450 g)** with a box grater or mandoline. Place in a colander, sprinkle over some **sea salt** and allow to sit for 10–15 minutes. Rinse the zucchini and squeeze aggressively to remove as much liquid as you can. Place the zucchini in a bowl and mix with **2 tablespoons of good-quality pesto** and **3½ ounces (100 g) of crumbled goat's cheese**. Taste and season with **sea salt** and **black pepper** if needed.

Summer

Beet and ricotta

Grate **7 ounces (200 g) of cooked beet** and combine with **¾ cup (about 200 g) of ricotta, 1 tablespoon of grated pecorino** and **1 tablespoon of chopped chives**. Season with **sea salt** and **black pepper**.

Corn salsa

Barbecue or broil **2 corn cobs** until slightly charred on all sides. Slice the kernels off the cobs and combine with **1 finely sliced scallion, 3½ ounces (100 g) of finely chopped cherry tomatoes, 1 finely diced green or red chile** and a **big handful of finely chopped cilantro leaves**. Add the **zest of 1 lime** and season with **sea salt** and **black pepper**. If you like, add a **small handful of grated halloumi cheese**.

Tomato and egg

Whisk **4 large eggs**, season with **sea salt** and scramble. Remove from the pan and set aside. Blanch **1 pound (450 g) of tomatoes** for 30–60 seconds, then remove the skin and seeds and finely chop the flesh. Season the tomato with **sea salt** and drain in a colander for 10 minutes. Stir **2 teaspoons of brown sugar** through the tomato, then add to the scrambled eggs, along with **1 finely chopped scallion**. Taste and season with **sea salt** and **white pepper**.

Autumn

Carrot, kimchi and feta

Grate **2 small carrots (about 9 ounces / 255 g)** and sprinkle with **½ teaspoon of sea salt**. Place in a colander and allow to drain for 15 minutes. Rinse the carrot and squeeze out any excess moisture. Combine the carrot with a **heaped ½ cup (100 g) of vegan kimchi** and scatter in **3½ ounces (100 g) of crumbled feta**. Season with **sea salt** and **black pepper**.

Herby mushrooms

Heat a frying pan over medium heat and drizzle with **olive oil**. Add **1 finely chopped shallot** and cook for 1 minute. Add **9 ounces (255 g) of finely chopped mixed mushrooms** (I like oyster, shiitake and cremini) and **1 finely chopped garlic clove** and cook for 3–4 minutes until the mushrooms are wilted and golden. Remove from the heat. Stir in **2 tablespoons of dried breadcrumbs** and a **handful each of chopped dill, parsley and cilantro**. Season with **sea salt** and **black pepper**.

Butternut squash, chickpea and tahini

Combine **1 cup (225 g) of very soft cooked butternut squash** with **100 g (about ½ cup) cooked chickpeas**, **1 tablespoon of tahini** and **3 tablespoons of finely chopped walnuts**. Mash everything together, then add a **handful each of chopped parsley and chives**. Season with **sea salt** and **black pepper**.

Winter

Brussels sprouts, miso and sesame

Add a drizzle of **olive oil** to a frying pan, throw in **12 ounces (350 g) of finely chopped Brussels sprouts** and cook over medium–high heat for 2 minutes until softened. Add **2 finely chopped garlic cloves** and cook until the sprouts are completely soft. Turn off the heat and add **2 teaspoons of white (shiro) miso paste** and **1 teaspoon of toasted white sesame seeds**. Season with **black pepper**.

Lentil and cauliflower curry

Add a drizzle of **olive oil** to a frying pan, add **10½ ounces (300 g) of finely chopped cauliflower** and cook over medium–high heat for 2 minutes until softened. Add **1 finely chopped garlic clove**, **½ cup (100 g) cooked brown lentils** and **2 teaspoons of curry powder** and cook until the cauliflower is completely soft. Season with **sea salt** and **black pepper**. Remove from the heat and stir through a **handful of chopped cilantro leaves**.

Sweet potato and black olives

Cook **2 small sweet potatoes (about 12 ounces / 350 g)** until very soft. Scoop out the flesh and place in a bowl, along with a **big handful of chopped cilantro leaves** and **½ cup (90 g) of chopped black olives**. Taste and season with **sea salt** and **black pepper**.

Spring   **Summer**

Autumn　　　　　　　　　　　　　　　**Winter**

Simple vegan wontons

Wontons are an easy everyday food, especially when you have a ready-made batch in the freezer. My mother always made them in bulk and would pull them out of the freezer, a few at a time, for a quick meal. To prepare wontons for storage, line a tray with parchment paper and arrange the wontons in a single layer. Place them in the freezer and when they are hard, remove them from the tray, place in an airtight container and return to the freezer.

There are many ways to fold wontons—some are quite simple, while others take a bit of practice to master (search online for wonton-folding videos for a helpful visual). My mum's method is the traditional "Cantonese" or "Hong Kong" fold, where the filling is bundled up into a ball with ruffled edges. The simplest way is to fold the square wrapper in half to form a triangle. If you want to move to the next level, you can bring the two base corners together to form a "nurse's cap," or cross the corners over one another to form a fish shape (see image opposite). The wrappers dry out easily, so always cover both the wrappers and your completed wontons with damp tea towels.

MAKES ABOUT 45
VEGAN

14 ounces (400 g) extra-firm tofu, drained for 10 minutes

4 scallions, finely sliced

Handful of cilantro leaves, finely chopped

1 tablespoon tamari or soy sauce

2 teaspoons shaoxing rice wine

2 teaspoons toasted sesame oil

½-inch (1.25 cm) piece of ginger, peeled and finely chopped

1 garlic clove, finely chopped

½ teaspoon sugar

2 teaspoons cornstarch or potato starch

About 45 (3-inch / 7.5 cm) square vegan wonton wrappers

Sea salt

Crumble the tofu into a large bowl and add the scallions, cilantro, tamari or soy sauce, shaoxing rice wine, sesame oil, ginger, garlic, sugar and ½ teaspoon of sea salt. Mix, mashing the tofu, until well combined. Add the cornstarch or potato starch to absorb any excess moisture—if the mixture is still too wet, place in a colander and drain for a few minutes.

Place the wonton wrappers on your work surface and cover them with a damp tea towel. Hold a wrapper in the palm of your hand and place a teaspoon of filling in the center (don't add too much filling as the wonton will be hard to handle). Moisten the edge of the wrapper with a dab of water and carefully fold one corner over the filling to the opposing corner to form a triangle—make sure you enclose the filling tightly to avoid any air pockets which can make the wontons burst. Bring the two base corners together, dab one with water, then overlap them and press to seal. Repeat with the remaining wrappers and filling. At this point, you can freeze the wontons or cook them immediately.

Bring a large saucepan of salted water to the boil. Add a few wontons at a time and cook for 1–2 minutes, until they float to the top. Cook for another 20 seconds, until the skin is translucent, then remove immediately with a slotted spoon. Serve warm with your favorite broth, oil or dipping sauce.

Eat your wontons with

- Everything Oil (see page 25)
- Ginger–Scallion Oil (see page 28)
- Reliable Dumpling Dipping Sauce (see page 29)
- Red Curry Laksa Noodle Soup (see page 101)
- Ginger–Turmeric Broth (see page 103)

Nepalese ricotta and spinach momos with chile and tomato relish

When we lived in Sydney, we often visited a modest little restaurant called The Nepalese Kitchen, an institution in our local neighborhood. Inside, it was warm and familiar, with rich aromas of spice that hugged us as we entered. At that time, and perhaps still now, traditional Nepali food was hard to come by in Sydney. Their menu featured street-style snacks like pani puri (crispy bite-sized semolina puffs stuffed with potatoes and chickpeas), a curry made with nine different legumes called kwanti, and, of course, momos, Nepal's take on dumplings. It was here that I first tasted cheese in a dumpling. Filled with spinach and ricotta and served with a spicy, tangy achaar, it was an exciting interpretation of a food I knew so well. These momos are impossible not to love, a total crowd-pleaser and probably the dumplings I make more of than any other at home.

MAKES 20

5 ounces (140 g) baby spinach leaves

1 garlic clove, finely chopped

8 ounces (225 g) ricotta

¼ cup (30 g) grated pecorino

2 scallions, finely chopped

20 round store-bought or homemade dumpling wrappers (see page 112)

Sea salt and black pepper

Chile and tomato relish

1 teaspoon black or brown mustard seeds

Vegetable oil

1 pound (450 g) tomatoes, roughly chopped

1 teaspoon ground turmeric

2 garlic cloves, finely chopped

6 curry leaves (fresh or dried)

3 tablespoons tamarind purée, or more to taste

1 long red chile, roughly chopped

2 teaspoons sugar

1 teaspoon toasted sesame oil

Sea salt

Substitute

Spinach: kale or chard

Veganize

Use crumbled firm tofu instead of ricotta and pecorino

For the chile and tomato relish, place the mustard seeds in a frying pan, cover and dry-fry over medium heat until aromatic and the seeds have popped. Add a drizzle of vegetable oil to the pan, then add the tomatoes, turmeric, garlic, curry leaves and a pinch of sea salt and cook, covered, for 8–10 minutes, until the tomato mixture is thick and mushy. Stir in the tamarind, chile and sugar and cook over low heat for 5 minutes. Season with ½ teaspoon of sea salt. Take off the heat and stir in the sesame oil and 2 tablespoons of vegetable oil. Store in a sterilized jar in the fridge for up to 2 weeks.

In a large saucepan, add the spinach leaves, garlic, a pinch of sea salt and a splash of water. Cover and cook over medium heat until the spinach has wilted, about 2 minutes. Drain the spinach and allow it to cool, then squeeze it with your hands, wringing out as much liquid as possible.

Roughly chop the spinach and combine with the ricotta, pecorino and scallions. Season with sea salt and black pepper.

If you are using store-bought dumplings you will need to wet the edges, so set up a small bowl of water. With each wrapper, rotate the edge in the water until it is wet all the way around. If you are using homemade dumpling wrappers, there is no need to do this.

Hold a wrapper in the palm of your hand and place a small teaspoon of filling in the middle. Fold the wrapper over to form a half-moon shape, then, starting from one corner, pinch together and pleat until you get to the other corner. Gently flatten the dumpling to form a level bottom so they can sit upright.

As you finish each dumpling, place it on a sheet of parchment paper and cover with a damp tea towel to prevent them from drying out.

Place the momos in a steamer that has been lined with parchment paper or napa (Chinese) cabbage leaves. Cover and steam over a large saucepan of boiling water for about 10–15 minutes. Serve hot, with the chile and tomato relish.

Potato and leek momos

MAKES 16–18
VEGAN

1 pound (450 g) potatoes, peeled and cubed

Extra-virgin olive oil

1-inch (2.5 cm) piece of ginger, peeled and finely chopped

2 garlic cloves, finely chopped

1 leek, white and light green parts only, finely chopped

2 tablespoons chopped cilantro leaves

16–18 round store-bought or homemade dumpling wrappers (see page 112)

Sea salt and white pepper

Everything Oil (see page 25), Chile and Tomato Relish (see page 125) or your favorite hot sauce, to serve

Momos are Himalayan dumplings found in Tibet, Nepal and northern India. Usually steamed, they are also occasionally deep-fried, as they are at Phayul's, a fave Tibetan haunt in New York's Jackson Heights—their crispy potato momo is one of my constant cravings. As with all dumplings, you can fold these momos into any shape you like—these round ones take a bit of practice (I have yet to perfect my technique), but it's also fun to try new shapes. Momos are best served with something spicy.

Bring a large saucepan of salted water to the boil, add the potatoes and cook until completely soft. Drain and set aside to dry out for 3–5 minutes, then mash the potato.

In a large frying pan over medium heat, add a drizzle of oil, along with the ginger, garlic and leek, and season with sea salt and white pepper. Sauté, stirring constantly to prevent burning, for 3–4 minutes until the leek is translucent. Remove from the heat and stir in the mashed potato and cilantro. Taste and season with sea salt and white pepper.

If you are using store-bought dumplings you will need to wet the edges, so set up a small bowl of water. With each wrapper, rotate the edge in the water until it is wet all the way around. If you are using homemade dumpling wrappers, there is no need to do this.

Hold a dumpling wrapper in the palm of your hand and place a teaspoon of filling in the middle. Using the thumb and index finger of your other hand, pinch a portion of dough on one side to form a pleat. Make another pleat next to it, then continue pleating, rotating the dumpling slightly as you work your way around. Your pleats will eventually encase the filling. Gently twist the bottom of the dumpling in the opposite direction and make a small indentation in the center of the pleats with your thumb. (Alternatively, you could use the folding method in the ricotta and spinach momos on page 125, or your favorite dumpling folding method—any shape works.)

As you finish each dumpling, place it on a sheet of parchment paper and cover with a damp tea towel to prevent them from drying out.

Place the momos in a steamer that has been lined with parchment paper or napa (Chinese) cabbage leaves. Cover and steam over a large saucepan of boiling water for about 10–15 minutes.

Serve hot, with your choice of dipping sauce, relish or hot sauce.

Variation: You can also deep-fry your momos. Pour about 1 inch (2.5 cm) of high-temperature oil (such as vegetable or sunflower) into a small deep saucepan and heat over medium–high heat. Working in small batches, carefully drop in the momos and cook them on each side until they are golden all over, about 1–2 minutes. Remove and drain on paper towels.

Substitute

Potato: sweet potato

Leek: onion, shallot

Springtime rolls with miso–kale pesto

MAKES 12
VEGAN AND GLUTEN FREE

12 asparagus spears (about 5 ounces / 140 g), woody ends removed

3 ounces (85 g) snow peas, trimmed

3½ ounces (100 g) mung bean vermicelli, soaked in water for 15 minutes

Toasted sesame oil

12 (8-inch / 20-cm) rice paper rounds

12 romaine lettuce leaves

1 avocado, cut into thin wedges

Handful of mint leaves

Handful of cilantro leaves

Handful of basil or Vietnamese mint leaves

Sea salt

Miso–kale pesto

3½ ounces (100 g) kale leaves

½ cup (12 g) basil leaves

2 garlic cloves, roughly chopped

⅓ cup (45 g) toasted sunflower or pumpkin seeds

1 tablespoon white (shiro) miso paste

¾ cup (185 ml) extra-virgin olive oil

Zest and juice of ½ lemon

Sea salt and black pepper

If spring had a flavor, it would be these brightly herbaceous "spring" rolls. The asparagus, snow peas, lettuce and abundant herbs provide a fresh, crisp mouthful, perfect for a gathering or a fun roll-it-yourself midweek dinner for the family. Rice paper rolls are incredibly versatile—fill them with your favorite seasonal vegetables and add some pan-fried tofu if you're looking for protein. The miso–kale pesto dipping sauce makes the ideal companion; the miso adds a gentle umami, balancing perfectly with the earthy kale and sunflower seeds. If you're looking for a new go-to vegan pesto recipe, this is the one. It makes about 1 cup (250 g).

For the miso–kale pesto, bring a saucepan of well-salted water to the boil. Add the kale leaves and cook for 30–60 seconds, just until they are wilted and bright green. Remove from the water with tongs (keep the water for the other veggies), place in a colander and rinse under cold water. Drain, then squeeze out any excess water. Roughly chop the kale and place in a food processor or blender. Add the basil, garlic and seeds and whiz to a paste. Add the miso, then slowly drizzle in the olive oil, lemon juice and about 2 tablespoons of water and blend again until combined. Stir in the lemon zest and season with sea salt and black pepper, then set aside.

If your asparagus spears are long, snap them in half so they are about 4 inches (10 cm) in length. Bring the pan of salted water back to the boil, drop in the asparagus and snow peas and cook for about 1 minute until they are bright green. Remove from the water with tongs (keep the water for the vermicelli) and place in a colander, then immediately refresh under cold running water until completely cold. Add the mung bean vermicelli to the boiling water and cook for 1–2 minutes until completely transparent. Drain and rinse under cold water. Drizzle a little sesame oil over the vermicelli and season with a pinch of sea salt. Set aside.

To assemble the rolls, take a deep plate that is slightly larger than the rice paper rounds and pour in some lukewarm tap water. Working with one round at a time, dunk the rice paper into the water and allow to soften for 30–60 seconds—don't let it get too soft or it will break when rolling. When softened, lay it out flat on a cutting board and assemble your filling. Starting at the edge of the rice paper closest to you (and leaving enough room to begin the rolling process), layer a piece of lettuce, followed by a small handful of vermicelli, asparagus, snow peas, avocado and herbs. To roll, pull the edge closest to you over the filling—pull it tight to keep everything in place. Fold over once, then fold in the sides and continue to roll until you have a nice, tightly bound roll. Continue with the remaining wrappers and filling.

To serve, cut the rolls in half and serve with the miso–kale pesto.

Substitute

Mung bean vermicelli: rice vermicelli

Snow peas: sugar snap peas

Ketchup fried rice arancini

Arancini balls are a favorite in our house—what's not to love about creamy rice packed into spheres and fried until crispy? Italian arancini are traditionally stuffed with meat, peas or mozzarella, which becomes melty and oozy when fried. This arancini recipe represents a miscellany of cultural influences. I've used Chinese fried rice as the base, to which I've added ketchup in a nod to the Japanese East-meets-West dish omurice; finally, the rice is rolled into balls, then crumbed and fried just like arancini. This is a highly adaptable dish—stuff with mozzarella or cheddar cheese, or add gochujang or kimchi to the rice for a bit of spice. The egg-flour-breadcrumb task always feels like a big job, but workflow is key—set up three bowls, arranged in order of dipping, to make it more efficient. You can also make them in bulk, then freeze the fried arancini for up to a month and reheat in the oven to make them crispy again.

Heat a wok or large frying pan over medium–high heat. When hot, pour in a big drizzle of oil, then add the rice and fry, breaking it up with a spatula, for 2–3 minutes. Add the garlic, tamari or soy sauce and peas, and season with a few big pinches of sea salt. Toss well and fry for 2 minutes until the peas are cooked. Add the thinned ketchup and toss for 2 minutes until the rice is well coated. Transfer the rice to a large bowl, season with a few turns of black pepper and toss in the scallions. Taste and, if needed, season with a little more sea salt. Allow to cool for a few minutes.

Break one egg into the rice and, using your fingers or a large spoon, fold it through the rice. Shape the rice into 12 even spheres, each about the size of an oversized golf ball.

Set up your coating station. Beat the remaining eggs in a small bowl and season with sea salt and black pepper. In another bowl, add the rice flour, and in a third, the breadcrumbs. Coat each rice ball in flour, egg and then breadcrumbs.

Pour about 1½ inches (3.75 cm) of oil into a small, deep heavy-based saucepan and heat over medium–high heat until the oil is hot (test with a wooden spoon—if the oil sizzles, it is ready). Drop two or three arancini balls into the oil and fry for 2 minutes on each side, turning regularly until the balls are golden all over. Remove with tongs or a slotted spoon and drain on paper towels. Continue until all the balls are cooked.

Serve the arancini with your choice of dipping sauce.

MAKES 12
GLUTEN FREE

Vegetable, sunflower or other high-temperature neutral oil

4 heaped cups (about 28 ounces / 800 g) cooked brown or white rice (or a combination), preferably chilled in the fridge overnight

2 garlic cloves, finely chopped

1 tablespoon tamari or gluten-free soy sauce

1 cup (155 g) frozen peas

½ cup (125 ml) ketchup, thinned with 2 tablespoons water

2 scallions, finely sliced

3 large eggs

1 cup (175 g) rice flour

1 cup (110 g) dried gluten-free breadcrumbs

Sea salt and black pepper

Everything Oil (see page 25), Miso–Kale Pesto (see page 129) or Chile–Oat Crisp (see page 209), to serve

Substitute

Rice flour: all-purpose flour

Gluten-free breadcrumbs: regular dried or panko breadcrumbs

Crispy tofu and cilantro balls

At Kung Tak Lam Shanghai Vegetarian Cuisine restaurant, a looming high-rise restaurant overlooking Hong Kong's Causeway Bay, I sampled a dish of "tofu balls" that felt intensely familiar, almost personal, sparking a faint memory of a childhood food experience. While I can't quite recall where or when I'd previously eaten these fried tofu balls, it felt important to me, significant enough that this dish now regularly occupies my thoughts. My version pairs tofu with cilantro and five-spice powder, a happy marriage of aromatic flavors. The mixture is quite wet so be assertive when shaping them (or use a small ice-cream scoop to help form a ball). The potato starch gives them a nice crispy finish.

Place the tofu in a large bowl and mash it up with a fork. Add the cilantro, scallions, ginger, five-spice powder and eggs, and mix until well combined. Stir in the potato starch or cornstarch and season well with sea salt and white pepper. Shape into 15 golf ball–sized balls.

For the five-spice aïoli, combine all the ingredients in a small bowl.

Pour about 1½ inches (3.75 cm) of oil into a small, deep heavy-based saucepan and heat over medium–high heat until the oil is hot (test with a wooden spoon—if the oil sizzles, it is ready). Drop two or three balls into the oil and fry for 2 minutes on each side, turning regularly until the balls are golden all over. Remove with tongs or a slotted spoon and drain on paper towels. Continue until all the balls are cooked.

Serve the tofu balls with the aïoli and lemon wedges on the side.

MAKES 15
GLUTEN FREE

12 ounces (350 g) extra-firm tofu, well drained

½ cup (12 g) cilantro leaves, finely chopped

2 scallions, finely chopped

1-inch (2.5 cm) piece of ginger, peeled and finely chopped

½ teaspoon five-spice powder

2 large eggs, beaten

½ cup (60 g) potato starch or cornstarch

Vegetable, sunflower or other high-temperature neutral oil

Sea salt and white pepper

1 lemon, cut into wedges, to serve

Five-spice aïoli

½ cup (125 g) vegan or regular mayonnaise

½ teaspoon five-spice powder

1 teaspoon Sriracha or chile sauce

1 garlic clove, grated

Veganize

Replace the eggs with flax egg. To do this, combine 1 tablespoon of ground flaxseeds with 2½ tablespoons of water, then rest for 5 minutes. This will replace one egg, so double the quantities for these tofu balls.

Tofu "char siu" bao

Char siu bao, or barbecue pork bun, is a bona fide dim sum classic. The fluffy white buns come to the table in bamboo steamers, too hot to eat right away, but somehow best consumed this way. A burnt tongue is part of the char siu bao experience. Although preparing them requires a few steps, bao are quite simple to make at home. You can fill your bao with anything you like—try any of the dumpling fillings in this chapter.

MAKES 12

VEGAN

1 teaspoon active dry yeast

½ cup (100 g) sugar

1⅔ cups (250 g) all-purpose flour, plus extra for dusting

1 cup (125 g) potato starch or cornstarch

3 tablespoons vegetable or other neutral oil

2½ teaspoons baking powder

Sea salt

"Char siu" tofu filling

Vegetable or other neutral oil

1 onion, finely diced

10½ ounces (300 g) extra-firm tofu, drained and crumbled

2 tablespoons tamari or soy sauce

2 tablespoons kecap manis, sweet soy sauce or hoisin sauce

1 teaspoon sugar

1 teaspoon toasted sesame oil

½ cup (125 ml) vegetable stock or water

1 tablespoon potato starch or cornstarch, dissolved in 3 tablespoons water

1 scallion, finely chopped

Handful of cilantro leaves, roughly chopped

Sea salt and white pepper

In a large mixing bowl, dissolve the yeast and 1 tablespoon of the sugar in ¾ cup (185 ml) of warm water. Set aside for 5–10 minutes, until it looks a little bubbly.

Whisk together the flour, potato starch or cornstarch and ½ teaspoon of sea salt, then add to the yeast mixture, along with the oil and remaining sugar. Bring everything together with your hands, then knead in the bowl until the mixture comes together. Transfer to a lightly floured work surface and knead until smooth, about 2 minutes. Cover with a damp tea towel and let it rest for 2 hours.

While the dough is resting, make the char siu tofu filling. Heat a drizzle of vegetable oil in a wok or large frying pan over medium heat, add the onion and tofu and cook for about 5 minutes, turning every now and then, until the tofu is brown all over. Add the tamari or soy sauce, kecap manis, sweet soy or hoisin, sugar, sesame oil and stock or water, and season with white pepper. Add the potato starch or cornstarch slurry and stir constantly until thickened. Taste and season with a little sea salt and white pepper. Remove from the heat and stir in the scallion and cilantro. Chill in the fridge until you are ready to fill the bao.

After your dough has rested, flatten it with the palm of your hand to form an indent and add the baking powder. Knead until the dough is smooth (if it's hard to incorporate the baking powder because the dough is dry, sprinkle over 1–2 teaspoons of water). Cover with a damp tea towel and allow to rest for another 15–20 minutes.

Pour water into a saucepan that fits your bamboo or basket steamer and bring to the boil. Tear off some parchment paper and cut out 12 (4-inch / 10-cm) squares (or use flattened cupcake cases).

Roll the dough into one long tube, then cut it into 12 equal pieces. Working with one piece one at a time, roll it out to a 5-inch (12.5 cm) disc (you want the dough to be thicker in the middle and thinner at the edge). Place a tablespoon of filling in the center of the dough, and pleat the buns until they are sealed on top. There are many ways to pleat— the easiest way is to simply gather it up like a money bag and press to enclose, flattening the bottom so it sits flat. Sit each bun on a square of parchment paper and place inside your steamer. Steam in two or three batches (keep the remaining bao covered under a damp tea towel).

Keeping the pan of water at a rolling boil, carefully place the steaming basket on top and cover with the lid. Steam over high heat for 10–12 minutes, until the buns are plump. Eat them warm.

Note: This dough can also be mixed in a stand mixer fitted with a dough hook.

Mushroom and kimchi "sausage rolls"

Our childhood birthday parties were always slightly awkward. In lieu of party games or activities, my parents' one and only party trick was food. And lots of it. My mum and dad, not really attuned to the customs of Western-style children's birthdays, would fill our sprawling dining table with plate after plate of food: Chinese roast pork, Kentucky Fried Chicken, hot dogs (which we would dip in soy sauce and white pepper), spring rolls, prawn crackers and chicken wings. A haphazard array of food that somehow kept the mini-masses happy. Along with the fancy food, humble party pies and sausage rolls were also celebration staples. This recipe is my West-meets-East homage to an Aussie party food classic—mushroom and kimchi "sausage rolls," served with ketchup, of course. An assured crowd-pleaser, they are meat-free yet "meaty," suitable for those who love the undeniable appeal of bite-sized pastry filled with umami goodness.

MAKES 28

Olive oil

1 leek, white part only, finely sliced

1 garlic clove, finely chopped

1 pound (450 g) cremini mushrooms, finely chopped

2 thyme sprigs, leaves picked

1 cup (200 g) store-bought or homemade kimchi (see pages 38–39)

½ cup (50 g) dried breadcrumbs

1 cup (125 g) grated sharp cheddar

2 teaspoons Dijon mustard

Handful of soft herbs (parsley, dill, chives) and/or scallion, finely chopped

2 (10-inch / 24 cm) square sheets frozen puff pastry, thawed

1 large egg, beaten

2 teaspoons sesame seeds (white, black or a combination)

Sea salt and black pepper

Ketchup, to serve

Substitute

Cremini mushrooms: shiitake or button

Cheddar: Parmesan or pecorino

Veganize

Replace the cheddar with grated vegan cheese or crumbled firm tofu, along with a tablespoon of nutritional yeast

Use vegan puff pastry and brush the pastry with melted vegan butter, rather than egg

Preheat the oven to 400°F (200°C). Line a large sheet pan with parchment paper.

Heat a drizzle of oil in a large frying pan over low heat, add the leek, garlic and a good pinch of sea salt and cook for 10 minutes, until very soft and sweet. Add the mushrooms and thyme, then increase the heat to medium–high and cook for 6–8 minutes, until the mushrooms are soft and starting to caramelize. Season with sea salt and black pepper, then scoop into a large mixing bowl.

Squeeze out all the moisture from the kimchi and finely chop. Add the kimchi, breadcrumbs, cheddar and mustard to the mushroom mixture and stir to combine. Mix through the herbs, then taste, and season with sea salt and black pepper if needed. Set aside to cool slightly.

Take one sheet of pastry and cut it in half to make two rectangles. Spoon one-quarter of the mushroom mixture along the middle of one length of pastry, molding it into a sausage shape. Brush the beaten egg along one pastry edge, then fold the pastry over to enclose the filling, pressing it into the eggwashed edge. Turn it over so that the seam is on the bottom. Repeat with the remaining pastry and filling, until you have four long rolls. Cut each roll into seven bite-sized pieces.

Place the rolls on the prepared sheet pan, brush with the eggwash and sprinkle with sesame seeds. Bake for 18–20 minutes, or until golden. Serve with ketchup.

Store leftover rolls in an airtight container in the freezer for up to 3 months.

Rice is gold and all the things to eat with it

The rice legacy

Rice is to Asians what bread is to the French. Without rice, a meal is not complete. In Cantonese, we are called to the table with the words "sikh fan" which translates to "eat rice." Similarly, in Thailand, you don't ask friends if they've had dinner yet, you ask, "Kin khao ayung?" meaning "have you had rice yet?" and in Korean, bap means both "rice" and "food" (or "meal"). In Asian culture, rice is the most prized item on the table. Every side dish is made to complement the rice. It is our constant, our comfort, our survival. We cannot feel fully satiated without it.

As a child, rice was our dinnertime ritual. My mother served a traditional Cantonese banquet every night—soup, followed by rice served with a variety of meats and vegetables. Dinner was hearty and heavy, and no matter how many of the side dishes we ate, we always needed to finish our rice. Every single grain. Dinner was a balancing act, where timing and rhythm was key—we needed to resist the temptation to eat too fast because once our bowl of rice was empty, it was a sign that we were replete, and it was time to leave the table. In our house, to stay and eat the side dishes, without rice in our bowls, was seen as impolite.

The making of rice is simple, just rice and water. My mother always used a rice cooker, a permanent fixture in her kitchen. She washed and rinsed the rice at least three times, vigorously rubbing it to get rid of the starch, thereby preventing clumps and giving a fluffier result. My mother never measured her ratio of rice to water. She taught me the classic Chinese method of measuring the water with our fingers. Some call this the "first knuckle method;" it involves touching our index finger to the surface of the rice and adding water until it just reaches the first crease (or knuckle) on our finger. Over the years, I've heard from friends that their Asian mums had similarly unconventional ways of measuring rice water—some place their palm flat on the rice, adding water until it rises to the first crease in their wrist. The "first knuckle method" is usually met with understandable skepticism; after all, everyone has different sized fingers and no two knuckles are the same. It defies logic, yes. But for me, whether I'm using a rice cooker, donabe (Japanese claypot) or cast-iron pot, this method just works. While modern cooking can be an applied science, with copious rules and predicted outcomes, there is also so much to learn from the way our mothers, grandmothers and their ancestors cooked. More often than not, these heirloom cooking techniques are based upon generations of tradition, born from *feeling* food rather than thinking about it. So, for me, with the legacy of rice coursing through my veins, I just know that my finger will always give me the most perfect bowl of rice.

Green beans with black bean sauce

Fermented black beans are an umami bomb. Much like olives or Parmesan, the flavor is intoxicating, so intensely savory and salty that you immediately crave more. Fermented black beans (or dou chi) are actually black soybeans that have been fermented and salted, making them soft and semidry. Growing up, fermented black beans were one of my favorite flavors—in my meat-eating youth, I often requested my mother's steamed pork cakes, laced with dou chi. At the supermarket, you will most likely find black bean sauce, a spicy, addictively flavorful sauce that you can add to stir-fries and greens. You can use Chinese spicy black bean sauce in this recipe, but if you happen to find a bag of fermented black beans (probably in an Asian grocer) then please try this homemade version, which has a much fresher taste. Double the recipe, as this sauce keeps well in the fridge.

SERVES 4, WITH RICE
VEGAN

Vegetable oil

9 ounces (255 g) green beans, trimmed

1 tablespoon toasted white sesame seeds

Sea salt and black pepper, if needed

Homemade black bean sauce

½ cup (70 g) fermented black beans

2 garlic cloves, finely chopped

1 teaspoon red chile flakes

2 tablespoons shaoxing rice wine

2 teaspoons tamari or soy sauce

1 teaspoon sugar

2 tablespoons olive oil

For the black bean sauce, place the beans in a colander and rinse under cold running water. Drain well. Tip the beans into a small bowl and mash with the back of a fork or spoon to form a rough paste. Add the remaining ingredients and mix well.

Place a wok or large frying pan over high heat. When hot, add a good drizzle of oil and swirl the wok or pan to coat the surface. Add the green beans and cook for about 2 minutes. Add 2 tablespoons of black bean sauce, along with about 3 tablespoons of water, and toss for another 1–2 minutes, until the beans are bright green and tender-crisp. Taste and season with sea salt and black pepper if necessary—you could add more black bean sauce if you wish. Sprinkle with the sesame seeds and serve with rice.

Substitute

Homemade black bean sauce: store-bought black bean sauce

Green beans: zucchini, snake beans or broccoli

Red chile flakes: 1 long red chile, finely chopped

Replace shaoxing rice wine with dry sherry (or omit) for gluten free

Mapo tofu

A rich, spicy tofu stew, mapo tofu is comfort in a bowl. This is one of the first recipes my mother adapted for me when I became vegetarian. Her recipe includes pickled radish and a spicy bean paste called doubanjiang, but I've opted to use black bean sauce instead, which packs a similar punch and is slightly easier to find at supermarkets (or make your own with the recipe on page 143). Mapo tofu originally hails from Sichuan province, so authentic recipes contain both pork and a lot of mouth-numbing Sichuan peppercorns. My version is pretty mellow, but if you'd like to spice things up, simply drizzle with everything oil (see page 25) or chile oil when serving. And, of course, rice is mandatory.

Drain the mushrooms and squeeze out the water, then finely slice.

In a Dutch oven, flameproof casserole dish or saucepan, heat the oil over medium–low heat, add the black bean sauce, chile, garlic and ginger and cook, stirring, for 2 minutes. Add the mushrooms and carrot, then reduce the heat to very low and cook for another 2 minutes.

Add the tofu, vegetable stock, sugar and 1 teaspoon of sea salt, then very gently fold everything together—the tofu will naturally break up. Cover and bring to the boil, then reduce heat and cook for 5–7 minutes until the carrot is tender. Uncover, gently stir in the potato starch or cornstarch slurry and cook for 1 minute, until the sauce has thickened. Taste and season with sea salt and white pepper, as needed. Finally, add the peas and cook for another minute until they are just tender.

Remove from the heat immediately. Drizzle with sesame oil and scatter the scallions over the top. Serve with rice.

SERVES 4, WITH RICE
VEGAN

¾ ounce (21 g) dried shiitake mushrooms, soaked in hot water for 20 minutes

1 tablespoon vegetable or other neutral oil

1 tablespoon black bean sauce

1 long red chile, finely chopped (remove the seeds if you prefer less heat)

1 garlic clove, finely chopped

1-inch (2.5 cm) piece of ginger, peeled and finely chopped

1 carrot, peeled and diced

25 ounces (700 g) soft tofu, broken into large chunks

1 cup (250 ml) vegetable stock

1 teaspoon sugar

1 tablespoon potato starch or cornstarch, mixed with 1 tablespoon water

1 cup (155 g) frozen or fresh peas

Toasted sesame oil

2 scallions, finely chopped

Sea salt and white pepper

Substitute

Dried shiitake mushrooms: 2 ounces (60 g) fresh shiitake mushrooms

Black bean sauce: spicy bean paste (doubanjiang)

Cumin tofu stir-fry

SERVES 4, WITH RICE
VEGAN

Vegetable or other neutral oil

1 onion, finely sliced

½–1 long red chile, sliced diagonally
(remove the seeds if you prefer
less heat)

1-inch (2.5 cm) piece of ginger, peeled
and finely chopped

1 garlic clove, finely chopped

10½ ounces (300 g) cauliflower,
cut into florets

Big handful of cilantro leaves

1 tablespoon toasted white
sesame seeds

Sea salt

Marinated tofu

1 tablespoon tamari or soy sauce

1 tablespoon shaoxing rice wine

½ teaspoon sea salt

14 ounces (400 g) extra-firm tofu,
cut into ¾-inch (2-cm) cubes

3 tablespoons potato starch
or cornstarch

Spice mix

2 tablespoons ground cumin

2 teaspoons gochugaru (Korean red
chile flakes), red chile flakes or
Sichuan chile flakes

½ teaspoon sugar

½ teaspoon sea salt

Substitute

Cauliflower: mushrooms, broccoli
or eggplant

Replace shaoxing rice wine with dry
sherry or mirin for gluten free

While cumin is one of the most-used spices in my pantry, employing it in Chinese cooking is completely new to me. In Chinese cuisine, cumin imparts an abstract complexity which makes otherwise familiar dishes taste foreign. At Xi'an Famous Foods in New York, the unique cuisine of Xi'an in northwest China tastes unmistakably like the confluence of China and the Middle East. Dishes are heavily spiced with cumin, chile and Sichuan peppercorns, resulting in bold, not for the faint of heart flavors. I was particularly intrigued by the sound of their signature lamb dish, with chunks of meat dry-fried in a heavy cumin spice mix. This is my take on the dish, featuring tofu and cauliflower.

For the marinated tofu, combine the tamari or soy sauce, shaoxing rice wine and sea salt in a bowl. Add the tofu cubes and toss to coat. Allow to marinate at room temperature for 20–30 minutes.

Meanwhile, to make the spice mix, combine all the ingredients in a small bowl and set aside.

Drain the tofu. Place the potato starch or cornstarch in a deep bowl, add the marinated tofu cubes and toss gently to coat.

Heat a large frying pan over high heat; when hot, drizzle with oil and add the tofu cubes, arranging them in one layer. Reduce the heat to medium and allow the tofu to cook, undisturbed, for 1–2 minutes, until the bottom is golden. Flip the tofu over and cook until golden on all sides. Transfer the tofu to a plate lined with paper towels to drain. Wipe out the pan.

Add a little more oil to the pan, toss in the onion, chile, ginger and garlic and stir-fry for about 1 minute until fragrant. Add the cauliflower, season with sea salt and stir-fry for 4–6 minutes until the cauliflower is just tender. Add the tofu, along with the spice mix, and stir to combine. Take the pan off the heat.

Taste and season with a touch of sea salt if needed. Top with the cilantro and sesame seeds, then toss everything together and serve with rice.

Salt and pepper eggplant

Before I go home to visit, my mother and I talk on the phone about the food I want to eat when I arrive. My "off the plane" dish is always salt and pepper tofu. Pillows of tofu, gently fried until golden, scattered with chile and scallion seared in hot oil, and finished with a dusting of salt and pepper seasoning. This dish tastes like home.

In this recipe I use eggplant, which is an exciting variation on this classic dish. My mum and I love eggplant—for lunch, she would often steam fingers of eggplant and serve it with soy sauce and white pepper. This recipe is great because it is completely adaptable—in fact, I tried broccoli, cauliflower, green beans and asparagus before finally settling on eggplant. Any of those veggies will work and, of course, use chunks of firm tofu if you wish.

SERVES 4, WITH RICE
VEGAN AND GLUTEN FREE

1 eggplant (about 10½ ounces / 300 g), cut into ⅛-inch-thick (4 mm) rounds

1 tablespoon tamari or gluten-free soy sauce

½ cup (60 g) potato starch or cornstarch

Vegetable, sunflower or other high-temperature neutral oil

2 scallions, finely sliced

½–1 long red chile, chopped

Salt and pepper seasoning

½ teaspoon sugar

1 teaspoon white pepper

¼ teaspoon ground ginger

½ teaspoon five-spice powder

2 teaspoons sea salt

Place the sliced eggplant in a bowl, add the tamari or soy sauce and toss to coat. Leave to marinate for 5–10 minutes. The marinade also tenderizes the eggplant, reducing the cooking time.

To make the salt and pepper seasoning, combine all the ingredients in a small bowl.

Place the potato starch or cornstarch in a bowl. Drain the eggplant, then add to the bowl and toss until well coated.

Pour some oil into a small deep saucepan (about ½ inch / 1.25 cm deep) and heat over high heat until hot (test with a wooden spoon—if the oil sizzles, it is ready). Working with a few slices at a time, add the eggplant and fry, turning, until both sides are golden. Remove with tongs or a slotted spoon and drain on paper towels.

Place the eggplant on a plate, sprinkle over some of the salt and pepper seasoning and toss to coat the eggplant. (Any leftover seasoning will keep in an airtight jar for several months.) Top with scallions and chile, and serve with rice.

Substitute

Eggplant: tofu, broccoli, cauliflower, green beans or asparagus

Potato and chive omelet

SERVES 4, WITH RICE
GLUTEN FREE

Olive oil

1 large potato (about 10½ ounces / 300 g), peeled and julienned

½ teaspoon sugar

2 ounces (60 g) garlic chives, cut into 1-inch (2.5 cm) lengths

5 large eggs, beaten

Sea salt and black pepper

Potato omelet is one of my mother's quick midweek staples. Similar in vibe to a Spanish tortilla, but with much less technique, this effortless omelet features thin strips of potato, which are pan-fried until tender and then smothered in beaten egg. It's a rustic dish, so don't worry about trying to keep the omelet in one piece. Ultimately, this is the kind of food you can make without thinking; a repertoire dish you can rely on. It's also a great blank canvas for adding other veggies— my mother often added peas, corn, diced carrot or sliced onion.

Heat a good drizzle of oil in a large nonstick frying pan over medium– high heat. Add the potato, sugar and ½ teaspoon of sea salt, then reduce the heat to medium and cook for 6–7 minutes, moving the potato around constantly. When the potato is tender, add the garlic chives and cook for 2 minutes, or until softened.

Using a spatula or wooden spoon, flatten the potato mixture into an even layer. Add a little more oil, then pour the egg over the potato and tilt the pan back and forth to distribute it evenly. Season with a little sea salt and black pepper, then cook over medium–low heat for another 2–3 minutes until the bottom is set. Flip the omelet over, either in one piece or a section at a time, and cook until just set. Remove from the pan and serve over rice.

Substitute

Potato: cabbage, carrot or sweet potato

Garlic chives: chives

Stir-fried salt and vinegar potato

SERVES 4, WITH RICE
VEGAN AND GLUTEN FREE

2 large potatoes (about 22 ounces / 615 g), peeled and julienned

2 tablespoons toasted sesame oil or Everything Oil (see page 25)

2–4 dried red chiles (remove the seeds if you prefer less spice)

2 garlic cloves, finely chopped

½ green bell pepper, finely sliced

2 tablespoons tamari or gluten-free soy sauce

1 tablespoon malt, white or apple cider vinegar

Sea salt and white pepper

This is a mash-up of three dishes—Tibetan alu sipsip (spicy sliced potatoes), Sichuan-inspired vinegary stir-fried potatoes, and salt and vinegar chips. Dearly beloved S & V chips may seem an unusual inspiration for a stir-fry, but salt and acid is a solid flavor profile that works really well with stir-fried potatoes. This recipe also shows the versatility of potatoes beyond roasting and mashing—in many Asian cultures it's very common to eat potatoes with rice (see my mum's potato and chive omelet recipe on page 151). Slice your potatoes as uniformly as possible to ensure even cooking (use a mandoline if you wish). The potato strips remain quite crispy after cooking, almost tender-crisp, like asparagus or sugar snap peas. Make sure you rinse the sliced potato thoroughly before cooking as this will remove some of the starch, which would otherwise make the potato gluey.

Rinse the potato matchsticks under cold running water to remove the excess starch (keep going until the water runs somewhat clear). Drain them very well.

In a wok or large frying pan over medium–high heat, add the oil and chiles and toss together for 30 seconds. Add the potato matchsticks, garlic and bell pepper and stir-fry for 5–6 minutes until the potato is just soft, but still with a little crunch. Remove from the heat and add the tamari or soy sauce and vinegar, then season well with sea salt and white pepper. Serve with rice.

Substitute

Dried red chiles: ¼–½ teaspoon red chile flakes

Ginger–scallion miso-glazed eggplant

SERVES 4, WITH RICE
VEGAN AND GLUTEN FREE

4 Japanese eggplants (about 1 pound / 450 g), halved lengthwise

1 tablespoon toasted sesame oil

1 scallion, finely chopped

Handful of cilantro leaves

Ginger–scallion miso glaze

1 tablespoon white (shiro) miso paste

1 teaspoon sugar

3–4 tablespoons Ginger–Scallion Oil (see page 28), plus extra to serve (optional)

2 teaspoons toasted white sesame seeds

Miso eggplant, or nasu dengaku, is a charming seasonal Japanese dish of creamy broiled eggplant brushed with a sweet miso glaze. Here I give it my own spin with the addition of my favorite ginger–scallion oil, lending a lovely hint of herbaceous heat to the dish. The eggplant is cooked twice; it is roasted until tender and then glazed and broiled until slightly caramelized. Watch it like a hawk while it's broiling, as the miso glaze will burn quickly. Use Japanese eggplant (which is sometimes called Chinese eggplant) if you can find it—it is slightly sweeter, with a thinner skin and also has fewer seeds. Of course, you can also use regular globe or Italian eggplants—just cut a large eggplant into thick slices and cook it the same way.

Preheat the oven to 375°F (190°C).

Place the halved eggplants, cut-side up, on a large sheet pan and brush with the sesame oil. Roast for 20–25 minutes until the eggplant is tender. Remove and allow to cool slightly.

Arrange a rack in the upper third of your oven and switch the heat to the "broil" setting.

For the glaze, whisk together the miso paste, sugar and 2 tablespoons of water until smooth. Stir in the ginger–scallion oil and half the sesame seeds.

Smear a generous amount of the glaze over each eggplant slice. Return to the oven and broil for 3–4 minutes until golden and starting to caramelize (watch the eggplant closely to prevent burning).

Scatter with the scallion, cilantro and remaining sesame seeds. Serve with rice and more ginger–scallion oil on the side, if you like.

Substitute

Japanese eggplants: regular eggplant (sliced) or zucchini

Black pepper Brussels sprouts with cold silken tofu

SERVES 4, WITH RICE
VEGAN

12 ounces (350 g) Brussels sprouts, trimmed and halved

Olive oil

1 (14-ounce / 400-g) block silken tofu

1 scallion, finely sliced

Handful of cilantro leaves

Sea salt

Black pepper sauce

2 tablespoons vegetable oil

2 garlic cloves, finely chopped

1-inch (2.5 cm) piece of ginger, peeled and finely chopped

2 shallots, finely sliced

2 long red chiles, finely chopped (remove the seeds if you prefer less heat)

3 tablespoons kecap manis or sweet soy sauce

2 tablespoons tamari or soy sauce

1 tablespoon dark soy sauce (optional)

2 teaspoons brown sugar

2 teaspoons freshly ground black pepper, plus extra if needed

Substitute

Long red chiles: red chile flakes, to taste

Use gluten-free soy sauces for gluten free

This dish is inspired by Japanese hiyayakko, cold tofu topped with soy sauce, grated ginger, scallions and shiso—a really excellent meal to eat on a warm day. Cold tofu delivers a refreshing touch to the table, a lovely contrast of temperature when served with hot rice or a rich, opulent sauce. This deeply decadent black pepper sauce is salty, sweet and spicy, a formidable counterpart to the earthy Brussels sprouts. This lively melange of intriguing, big-hitting flavors perfectly complements the neutrality of the cold silky tofu.

Preheat the oven to 400°F (200°C).

Place the Brussels sprouts on a sheet pan and drizzle with olive oil. Season with sea salt and roast for 25–30 minutes until golden and crispy.

Line a plate with a few sheets of paper towels and very gently place the tofu on top to drain for about 5 minutes.

Meanwhile, for the black pepper sauce, heat the oil in a frying pan over low heat, add the garlic, ginger, shallots and chile and cook for 5–6 minutes, stirring now and then, until everything is soft and sweet. Stir in the sauces and brown sugar, then add the black pepper. Taste and add more pepper if needed.

Remove from the heat and add the Brussels sprouts to the black pepper sauce. Stir in the scallion.

Place the block of silken tofu on a serving plate and spoon over the black pepper Brussels sprouts. Sprinkle with cilantro leaves and serve with rice.

Restaurant greens

When we go for dim sum with my mum, we are never allowed to order the restaurant greens. My mother, proudly frugal, always declares this dish a "rip off," routinely muttering in Cantonese, "why would I pay eight dollars for this dish when I can buy that bunch of greens for seventy-five cents?" Around the table, we give a perfunctory chuckle, and stare longingly at the plate of greens being placed on the table next to us. Growing up, I found my mother's thriftiness slightly maddening, but her words stuck (as they always do). As an adult, however much I might crave that plate of greens at dim sum, I can never bring myself to order it. Instead, I make it at home with this recipe.

As simple as this dish is, it does require discipline, assertiveness and swiftness when it comes to blanching the greens—it is essential that the leaves are just tender. The "greenness" is achieved by adding a touch of oil to the blanching water, an old trick my mother taught me years ago—the oil coats the vegetables, keeping them looking fresh and green. You could use any Asian greens for this recipe: choy sum, gai lan (Chinese broccoli), bok choy, baby bok choy, tatsoi, or any green leafy vegetables.

SERVES 4, WITH RICE
VEGAN

2 tablespoons vegetarian stir-fry sauce

½ teaspoon sugar

Big pinch of white pepper

1 bunch of your favorite Asian greens (about 12 ounces / 350 g)

Vegetable or olive oil

Sea salt

Garlic oil (optional)

3 tablespoons vegetable or olive oil

1–2 garlic cloves, finely chopped or sliced

If you are serving this with the garlic oil, heat the oil in a small saucepan over medium heat, and when hot (but not sizzling), add the garlic. Simmer for 10 seconds—as soon as the garlic starts to color, remove the pan from the heat. The garlic will continue to cook in the residual heat and turn a deeper shade of brown. At this point, you can strain the oil to remove the garlic for a smooth garlic oil, or just use the oil with the garlic in it. I prefer the latter.

Combine the vegetarian stir-fry sauce, sugar, white pepper, ½ teaspoon of sea salt and 2 tablespoons of hot water in a bowl and stir until well combined and the sugar has dissolved.

Wash the greens well to remove any dirt. If you are using long-stemmed leaves, cut them in half, separating the stems and leaves. If you are using smaller leaves, like baby bok choy, you can cook them whole. Bring a large saucepan of well-salted water to the boil. Add 1 teaspoon of oil, then drop the stems into the water first; cook for 10 seconds, then add the leaves. Using chopsticks or a wooden spoon, push and move the greens around the water so they are submerged and blanch for another 10 or so seconds. The exact cooking time will depend on the quantity and size of your greens, but stop cooking as soon as they are wilted and bright green. Pour into a colander and drain well.

Arrange the greens on a plate. (If you are not eating them immediately, submerge them in an ice bath to keep them green.) Drizzle over the sauce and top with a spoonful of garlic oil, if using. Serve with rice.

Substitute

Vegetarian stir-fry sauce: tamari for gluten free

Peppery bean sprouts with tofu

SERVES 4, WITH RICE
VEGAN AND GLUTEN FREE

Vegetable or olive oil

14 ounces (400 g) extra-firm tofu, drained and cut into ½-inch-thick (1.25 cm) slices

2 ounces (60 g) garlic chives, trimmed and cut into 1-inch (2.5 cm) lengths

1 garlic clove, finely chopped

1-inch (2.5 cm) piece of ginger, peeled and finely chopped

1 tablespoon tamari or gluten-free soy sauce

10½ ounces (300 g) bean sprouts

2 teaspoons white pepper, plus extra to serve

1 tablespoon toasted sesame oil

Sea salt

Where I live in Brooklyn, there is an Italian restaurant on almost every block (exaggerating, but you get my drift). And then there is Ugly Baby, an unassuming restaurant that manages to consistently attract an impressive out-of-the-neighborhood crowd with its brutally spicy Thai specialties. Indeed, eating at Ugly Baby requires endurance; the food ranges from hot to blazing to downright fiery, but if you can get past the flames you'll find some of the most delicious food I have tasted in New York. Our whole family loves Ugly Baby. We can't handle the heat of many dishes, but one of our favorites is a mellow, charmingly plain dish called pad tua ngok rau kao, which comes as a big mound of peppery bean sprouts (the menu specifies that it is made with stir-fried pork, but if you ask nicely they will make you a vegetarian version with tofu). This is my take on it—a simple stir-fry of bean sprouts, garlic chives and tofu, accentuated with a confident amount of white pepper.

Heat a large nonstick frying pan over medium–high heat. Add a drizzle of oil, then place the tofu slices in the pan, season well with sea salt and cook until golden, about 2–3 minutes. Flip the slices over and repeat on the other side. Remove from the pan and set aside to cool, then slice into thin strips.

Heat another splash of oil in the pan. When hot, reduce the heat to medium, add the garlic chives, garlic, ginger and tamari or soy sauce and toss for 30 seconds. Add the tofu strips, bean sprouts and white pepper and season with sea salt. Cook until the sprouts are slightly wilted but still crunchy, about 1–2 minutes, then take the pan off the heat. Drizzle in the sesame oil and toss to coat.

Taste and, if you like, dust with a little more white pepper. Serve with rice.

Substitute

Garlic chives: 4 scallions, finely sliced

Tamari: a few splashes of Maggi Seasoning Sauce

Bean sprouts: soybean sprouts

Ong choy with miso

Ong choy, otherwise known as water spinach, kangkung or water morning glory, is not your everyday vegetable. You won't be able to find it at your local supermarket, but it is readily available from most Asian grocers. I wanted to include this recipe because it is my favorite Asian green of them all. Ong choy is unique—the stems are hollow, the leaves are tender and, when stir-fried, it is full of texture. In Cantonese cuisine, there is a well-loved dish of stir-fried ong choy with garlic, chile and fermented bean curd. Fermented bean curd is a delicacy and an acquired taste (the flavor can best be described as "funky"), often used in stir-fries to deliver a salty-sweet depth to vegetables. In Malaysian cuisine, there is a similar dish called kangkung belacan, where the greens are cooked with shrimp paste.

This recipe offers a small twist on this Asian classic—my version uses miso, which offers a rich saltiness that is almost identical to fermented bean curd. I encourage you to try it even if you can't find ong choy—use spinach, amaranth leaves, snow pea shoots or choy sum instead. If you want an adventure, try cauliflower or eggplant in place of the greens; just be sure to adjust the cooking times accordingly.

SERVES 4, WITH RICE
VEGAN AND GLUTEN FREE

Vegetable or other neutral oil

2 garlic cloves, finely chopped

1 bird's eye or long red chile, finely chopped (remove the seeds if you prefer less heat)

1 pound (450 g) ong choy, cut into 3-inch (7.5 cm) pieces

2–3 heaped teaspoons white (shiro) miso paste

Sea salt

Heat a drizzle of oil in a wok or large frying pan over high heat. When the oil is hot, reduce the heat to medium, add the garlic and chile and cook for 10 seconds. Add the ong choy, 1–2 tablespoons of water and a big pinch of sea salt. Stir-fry for 2–3 minutes until the greens are wilted, then remove from the heat. Stir through the miso paste until it is melted through the greens, then serve with rice.

Substitute

Miso paste: fermented bean curd, salted black beans, black bean sauce (store-bought or homemade, see page 143), spicy bean paste (doubanjiang)

Ong choy: spinach, amaranth leaves, snow pea shoots, choy sum

Steamed "water egg" custard

It may come as a surprise that a recipe with three ingredients (one of which is water) has been the bane of my culinary life. In Cantonese, we call this dish "water egg"—egg whisked with water and a dab of salt, then steamed until it becomes a smooth, soft savory custard. I loved this dish when I was growing up, and I still do. My mother made it with dried scallops and we devoured it spooned over white rice. I always thought this dish was one of my mother's easier recipes, but when I tried to make it for myself, I was met with failure, time and again. Where my mother's steamed water egg was silky and light, mine was puffy and clumpy. Her custard was more baby's bottom, mine more wrinkly face. When I finally cracked it, the answer was actually in a small-but-mighty detail my mother had mentioned countless times—low heat, slow cooking time. In the end, the quest to perfect this three-ingredient recipe taught me a great deal: the importance of listening, the power of patience and that Mum is always right.

A smooth slippery texture is key to this dish. Using cooled, boiled water is important as this helps it combine with the egg. The water should not be hot at all; it should be warm, similar to tepid tap water.

This savory egg custard can be served however you like. A simple topping is soy sauce, sesame oil and sliced scallions or cilantro. You could also top it with ginger–scallion oil (see page 28) or an aromatic oil like my everything oil (see page 25), or enjoy it, unadorned.

SERVES 4, WITH RICE
GLUTEN FREE

2 large eggs

½ cup (125 ml) boiled water, cooled until it's just warm (not hot) to the touch

Sea salt

Topping options

Sliced scallion

Handful of cilantro leaves

Toasted sesame oil

Toasted white sesame seeds

Ginger–Scallion Oil (see page 28)

Everything Oil (see page 25)

Beat the eggs in a mixing bowl until the whites and yolks are completely blended. Place the bowl on a tea towel (to stop it from moving around) and slowly add the water in a steady stream, whisking constantly. Add ½ teaspoon of sea salt and whisk vigorously until the mixture is very well combined.

Place a steaming rack or trivet in a saucepan (make sure it will hold the bowl you will steam the custard in), then add water until it is just underneath the rack. Bring the water to the boil.

Pour the egg mixture through a sieve into a shallow heatproof bowl (the one I use is about 7 inches [17.5 cm] wide). Once the water has reached a rolling boil, place the bowl on the steaming rack or trivet. Cover with a lid, and immediately reduce the heat to the lowest temperature possible. Allow to steam for about 10 minutes, then lift the lid to see if the egg has set in the middle. If not, cover again and steam for another minute or so until it is set with a slight wobble. When the egg is ready, turn off the heat and leave the egg to sit, covered, for 5 minutes before removing.

Serve warm just as is, or with your chosen toppings, but always with rice.

Finger-lickin' good edamame beans with fried curry leaves

SERVES 4, WITH RICE
VEGAN AND GLUTEN FREE

Vegetable or other neutral oil

15–20 fresh curry leaves

1 tablespoon tamarind purée

1 tablespoon gluten-free sweet soy sauce

¼ teaspoon sugar

1 pound (450 g) frozen edamame beans in their pods, thawed for 20 minutes

Sea salt

Lime wedges, to serve

Spice paste

2 garlic cloves, roughly chopped

1 shallot, roughly chopped

½-inch (1.25 cm) piece of ginger, peeled and roughly chopped

⅛–¼ teaspoon red chile flakes

Edamame beans in their pods are the consummate pre-dinner snack at Japanese restaurants, but at home this can be a deeply satisfying with-rice dish. My favorite part of eating edamame is popping the entire pod into my mouth to drag the beans out with my teeth, savoring the sea salt flakes and any sauce coating the skin. This recipe is built upon this primal experience, of eating with your fingers, of popping an entire piece of food into your mouth, of spitting out the skin, of licking your fingers afterwards. The sticky, sweet, sour sauce is full of punch and life, and pairs perfectly with rice. The curry leaves add a lovely textural component to the dish, but you can leave them out without compromising on flavor.

For the spice paste, pound all the ingredients with a mortar and pestle, or blend in a food processor until it forms a chunky paste. Set aside.

In a wok or large frying pan over medium–high heat, add 3 tablespoons of oil. When hot, add the curry leaves and fry until crisp (this will only take a few seconds). Remove with tongs and drain on paper towels.

In the same oil, add the spice paste and fry, stirring constantly to prevent burning, for 1–2 minutes until soft and aromatic. Reduce the heat to low, add the tamarind, sweet soy sauce and sugar and simmer for another minute until syrupy. Add the edamame pods and toss to coat them in the sauce. Season with 1–2 pinches of sea salt. Top with the fried curry leaves and serve with rice and lime wedges.

Substitute

Gluten-free sweet soy sauce: tamari, soy sauce, kecap manis or liquid aminos

Steamed tofu and shiitake mushrooms with ginger, scallion and soy

SERVES 4, WITH RICE
VEGAN

14 ounces (400 g) firm tofu, cut into ½-inch-thick (1.25 cm) slices

2–3 fresh shiitake, oyster or trumpet mushrooms (about 3 ounces / 85 g), sliced

2 tablespoons tamari or soy sauce

1 tablespoon shaoxing rice wine

1-inch (2.5 cm) piece of ginger, peeled and julienned

1 scallion, julienned

Small handful of cilantro leaves

3 tablespoons vegetable or other neutral oil

Substitute

Tofu: eggplant

Omit the shaoxing rice wine for gluten free

On Friday nights, fresh from a day picking up seafood from the markets, my mother cooked fish for dinner. A whole steamed flounder or snapper, topped with scallion and ginger, then doused with hot oil to release the flavor of the aromatics into the flesh of the fish. I remember dreading "Fish Friday"—the pungent smell assaulted all my senses. The one saving grace was the sauce—soy sauce, oil, ginger and scallion. I would dip every mouthful of fish into the sauce and then spoon more sauce over my rice. It made everything better.

This recipe is made exactly the way my mother steamed her Friday fish, using tofu and shiitake mushrooms instead. Make sure you spoon the soy sauce and oil over white rice for the full effect.

Place a steamer basket or trivet in a wok or large saucepan, then pour in some hot water. Make sure the water does not touch the bottom of the steamer or trivet. Bring the water to the boil over high heat.

Lay the tofu slices in a single layer on a heatproof plate (make sure it fits into the steamer or on top of the trivet) and top with the mushrooms. Place the plate in the steamer or on the trivet, then cover and steam for about 5 minutes, or until the tofu is hot and the mushrooms are cooked. Carefully pour off some (but not all) of the liquid at the bottom of the plate.

While the tofu is steaming, stir together the tamari or soy sauce, shaoxing rice wine and 1 tablespoon of water. Set aside.

When the tofu and mushrooms are ready, very carefully remove the plate from the steamer or trivet. Lay the ginger, scallion and cilantro on top of the mushrooms.

Heat the oil in a small saucepan over high heat until it is hot but not smoking. Immediately remove the oil from the heat and very carefully (stand back as it will spit) pour it over the ginger, scallion and cilantro. Drizzle over the tamari or soy sauce mixture and serve with rice.

Braised lotus root, black fungus and vermicelli

I think of this dish as an abbreviated version of lo han jai, a vegan hotpot of braised vegetables that is sometimes called "Buddha's delight." We always ate this dish during the Lunar New Year, when my mother abstained from eating meat. My mother's lo han jai would include a long list of ingredients—shiitake mushrooms, bean curd sticks, fat choy (black moss), mung bean vermicelli, carrot, lotus root, wheat gluten, dried lily blossoms, black fungus, snow peas and baby corn. I always ate this dish with fermented bean curd, which would add a spicy, funky flavor to my bowl.

This recipe includes just a few of my favorite elements from lo han jai—lotus root (also known as renkon), black fungus (sometimes called wood ear mushrooms), water chestnuts and mung bean vermicelli. It's a simplified version, loaded with interesting textures. Lotus root, considered a lucky food in China and Japan, has a crisp texture even after cooking—if you can't find fresh lotus root, look for frozen packs at your Asian grocer. I've left the flavoring of this dish flexible—use black bean or chile bean sauce to inject a little spice, or hoisin for a smoother finish.

Heat a drizzle of oil in a deep frying pan or saucepan over high heat. Add the ginger, garlic and white part of the scallions and stir-fry for 30–60 seconds until aromatic. Drain the black fungus and add to the pan, along with the lotus root, water chestnuts, sugar and a pinch of sea salt, and stir-fry for 2 minutes.

Combine the vegetable stock with your choice of sauce. Drain the vermicelli. Add the stock mixture, vermicelli, tamari or soy sauce and sesame oil to the pan, then cover and cook for 3 minutes. Season with sea salt and white pepper. Top with the green part of the scallions and serve with rice.

SERVES 4, WITH RICE
VEGAN AND GLUTEN FREE

Vegetable or other neutral oil

1-inch (2.5 cm) piece of ginger, peeled and finely chopped

2 garlic cloves, finely chopped

2 scallions, white and green parts separated, roughly chopped

1 ounce (30 g) dried black fungus, soaked in hot water for 10 minutes

9 ounces (255 g) lotus root, sliced into ½-inch-thick (1.25 cm) discs

1 (5-ounce / 140-g) can water chestnuts, drained

½ teaspoon sugar

1 cup (250 ml) vegetable stock

2 teaspoons black bean sauce (store-bought or homemade, see page 143), spicy bean paste (doubanjiang), Everything Oil (see page 25), vegetarian stir-fry sauce or hoisin

2 ounces (60 g) mung bean vermicelli, soaked in water for 5–10 minutes

1 tablespoon tamari or gluten-free soy sauce

2 teaspoons toasted sesame oil

Sea salt and white pepper

Substitute

Black fungus: shiitake mushrooms

Salads for life

Finding empathy in salad

Growing up between two cultures, it took me a long time to understand the person I saw staring back at me in the mirror. But when I started cooking and, specifically, making salad, my own reflection suddenly made much more sense. Food became a gateway for me to understand my own heritage, while also offering a window into other cultures and their unique histories. Making salad with my mum brought us closer together; with cooking as our common ground, I felt like we were finally on the same side, that the disparate stories of our intertwined lives were finally being told on the same page.

Salad was not a part of my diet when I was a child, but it is the dish that has given me life.

Even today, nothing feels more natural than making a salad. In many ways, I equate salad making to living, to thriving, to being. Cooking has become important to me on so many levels. It nurtures the people I love, but it has also transformed the way I think, challenged the way I view the world and sparked my curiosity. In discovering flavor and experimenting with ingredients, I have become a more compassionate person, more worldly, better equipped to ask questions and to seek answers. No matter where we come from, food is our common language, a way to foster understanding, bring people together and, most of all, find empathy. In salads, we can make friends for life.

Smashed cucumber salad with tahini and spicy oil

SERVES 2–4
VEGAN AND GLUTEN FREE

6 Persian cucumbers, trimmed

1 tablespoon Everything Oil
(see page 25) or chile oil

2 teaspoons toasted sesame seeds
(white, black or a combination)

Handful of cilantro leaves

Sea salt and black pepper

Sesame dressing

2 tablespoons tahini

1 teaspoon toasted sesame oil

Sea salt and black pepper

This simple salad is great to serve as a snack or as a side to a bowl of noodles. Smashing the cucumbers tenderizes them, while a sprinkling of salt delivers a lovely pickle-like quality. In northern China, they serve a delicious smashed cucumber salad with vinegar, sesame oil and garlic. This version offers a surprising juxtaposition of texture and flavor—fresh, palate-cleansing cucumbers paired with an earthy sesame dressing, enlivened by a daring spicy oil.

To make the sesame dressing, whisk the tahini with 1–2 tablespoons of water until smooth. Add the sesame oil and stir until it's a thick pouring consistency (if it's too thick, add a little more water). Season with sea salt and black pepper.

Lay the cucumbers on a cutting board. Using the side of a wide knife or a rolling pin, gently smack the cucumbers until they break apart (be careful, otherwise they will fly off the board). Tear or cut into bite-sized pieces. Place the smashed cucumber in a colander and sprinkle with a pinch or two of sea salt. Allow to sit for 10 minutes to draw out any excess water. Drain off any liquid and pat dry with paper towels or a clean tea towel.

Place the cucumber on a plate and drizzle over the sesame dressing, followed by the everything or chile oil. Scatter with the sesame seeds and finish with the cilantro. Taste and, if needed, season with sea salt and black pepper.

Cucumber and cabbage noodle salad with black bean sauce

SERVES 4–6
VEGAN AND GLUTEN FREE

4 Persian cucumbers, trimmed

10½ ounces (300 g) thick rice noodles

½ small savoy or green cabbage (about 14 ounces / 400 g), finely sliced

3 tablespoons black bean sauce (store-bought or homemade, see page 143), or more to taste

2 tablespoons toasted sesame oil

Extra-virgin olive oil

½ lime

2 scallions, finely sliced

Handful of cilantro leaves or other Asian herbs (Vietnamese mint, shiso, Thai basil, etc.), roughly chopped

½ cup (75 g) roasted cashews, roughly chopped

Sea salt and black pepper

Substitute

Savoy or green cabbage: purple cabbage, napa (Chinese) cabbage or bean sprouts

Black bean sauce: spicy bean paste (doubanjiang), Everything Oil (see page 25) or chile oil

This salad is fresh and light, with a strong umami note from the black bean sauce. The contrast of slippery noodles teamed with crispy slivered cabbage is a familiar pairing in my Asian salad making; it is one of my favorite salad bases from which to build a story. The use of black bean sauce as a "salad dressing" has been a revelation for me. Far from my mother's Friday night special of stir-fried mussels (I never ate this as I really disliked the texture) or in her juicy steamed pork spare ribs, for me, fermented black beans are a powerful flavor builder in salads, in the ilk of olives, capers or hard cheese. If you have homemade or store-bought black bean sauce on hand, this salad can be ready in a flash.

Using a vegetable peeler, partially skin the cucumbers with vertical stripes. Halve the cucumbers lengthwise, use a teaspoon to scoop out the seeds, then slice the cucumbers diagonally.

Bring a large saucepan of salted water to the boil, add the rice noodles and cook according to the packet instructions until the noodles are just soft, about 6–7 minutes. Drain immediately and refresh under cold running water.

Place the noodles in a large bowl and add the cucumber, cabbage, black bean sauce, sesame oil and 2–3 tablespoons of olive oil. Squeeze over the lime juice, add half the scallions and herbs, and toss to coat everything thoroughly. Taste and season well with sea salt and black pepper and drizzle with more olive oil, if needed, to loosen up the noodles. Top with the cashews and remaining scallions and herbs and serve.

Roasted Brussels sprouts, chickpeas and edamame with ginger–scallion oil

SERVES 4-6
VEGAN AND GLUTEN FREE

1⅓ pounds (625 g) Brussels sprouts, trimmed and halved

1 pound (450 g) cooked chickpeas (about two 14-ounce / 400-g cans, drained)

9 ounces (250 g) frozen edamame beans

Olive oil

1 teaspoon ground coriander

About ½ cup (125 ml) Ginger–Scallion Oil (see page 28)

⅓ cup (50 g) toasted sesame seeds (white, black or a combination)

2 scallions, finely chopped

Handful of cilantro leaves

Sea salt and black pepper

Substitute

Brussels sprouts: broccoli, cauliflower or eggplant

Chickpeas: lentils, white beans or butter beans

When I'm not cooking for work, research or self-education, my diet is almost entirely driven by cravings. While often this means a longing for fries or cheese or anything deep-fried, at certain times of the month I just need to eat greens. When this happens, my body does not want light and airy salad greens; it yearns for a brassica, a leaf that is deeply earthy and somewhat bitter, like kale, broccoli or Brussels sprouts. This is a simple salad for days when only Brussels sprouts will satiate my green hunger. While golden, creamy sprouts are good enough to eat straight from the sheet pan, sometimes I muster the patience to turn them into this salad, where they are cleverly combined with two household staples—chickpeas and edamame— and dressed with my beloved ginger–scallion oil.

Preheat the oven to 425°F (220°C).

Place the Brussels sprouts, chickpeas and edamame beans on a large sheet pan and drizzle generously with olive oil. Sprinkle over the ground coriander and season well with sea salt and black pepper, then toss to coat. Roast for 25–30 minutes, until the sprouts are golden and tender and the chickpeas and edamame are slightly crispy.

Combine the Brussels sprouts, chickpeas and edamame beans in a large bowl. Add the ginger–scallion oil and half the sesame seeds and toss to mix everything together. Taste and season with sea salt and black pepper. Top with the scallions, cilantro leaves and remaining sesame seeds and serve.

Bánh mì salad

Bánh (bread) is a type of baguette introduced to Vietnam during the French occupation, but the bánh mì sandwich came to life after the French defeat, and in some ways encapsulates the end of colonialism there. While French-inspired, the sandwich is filled with the liveliness and spirit of Vietnam—protein such as grilled pork, pâté or tofu, emboldened by pickled veggies, lashings of mayonnaise and a brave handful of cilantro leaves.

Vietnamese bánh mì is as close to a salad as a sandwich is going to get. The bright flavors work wonderfully as a perky salad, brimming with contrasting textures and an impeccable balance of tart, sweet and salty.

SERVES 4
VEGAN

1 baguette or other loaf (about 5 ounces / 140 g), torn or cut into 1-inch (2.5 cm) chunks

Extra-virgin olive oil

14 ounces (400 g) extra-firm tofu, drained and cut into ⅛-inch-thick (4 mm) slices

1 long red or green chile, finely sliced

Big handful of cilantro leaves

Sea salt and black pepper

Quick pickles

1 cup (250 ml) apple cider vinegar

1 tablespoon sea salt

3 tablespoons sugar

2 garlic cloves, smashed

1 Persian cucumber, halved, seeds scraped out, then julienned

5½ ounces (155 g) daikon radish, peeled and julienned

2 small carrots, peeled and julienned

1 shallot or small red onion, finely sliced

Sriracha mayo

2 teaspoons Sriracha chile sauce

⅓ cup (80 g) vegan mayonnaise

1 scallion, finely chopped

Sea salt and black pepper

Preheat the oven to 400°F (200°C).

Lay the chunks of bread on a large sheet pan and drizzle with olive oil. Sprinkle with sea salt and toss with your hands to coat everything. Bake for 15–18 minutes, tossing the croutons halfway through to ensure they are evenly golden.

Meanwhile, prepare the quick pickles. Combine the vinegar, salt, sugar, garlic and ½ cup (125 ml) of water in a bowl and stir until the salt and sugar have dissolved. Add the cucumber, daikon, carrot and shallot or onion and mix thoroughly. Allow to pickle for 30 minutes, then drain the vegetables. Remove and discard the garlic.

Place a large frying pan over medium–high heat and add a drizzle of oil. Working in batches if necessary, add the tofu slices in a single layer and season very well with sea salt and black pepper. Pan-fry for 2–3 minutes until golden, then flip over and cook on the other side until golden. Continue until all the tofu is cooked. Remove and allow to cool, then slice into thin strips.

For the Sriracha mayo, whisk together the Sriracha, mayonnaise and scallion. Taste and season with sea salt and black pepper.

To serve, layer the croutons with the pickles and tofu strips, then top with a few spoonfuls of the Sriracha mayo, and toss. Finish with sliced chile, cilantro leaves and a small drizzle of oil.

Note: The drained pickles can be kept in the fridge for up to 3 days.

Substitute

Vegan mayonnaise: mayonnaise

Apple cider vinegar: rice vinegar or white wine vinegar

Daikon: radish or turnip

Bread: store-bought croutons

Grilled napa Caesar with wonton-scallion crackers

A vegetarian-style Caesar salad is a repertoire dish that I often serve when I'm looking for a quick, reliable meal to please the whole family. Here, I've given it the Asian treatment in a salad with three independently delicious parts that come together beautifully. The smoky and sweet grilled napa (Chinese) cabbage is a revelation, the scallion crackers made of wonton wrappers are highly addictive (finally, something to do with those stray wrappers in the fridge), and the creamy black bean Caesar dressing is brimming with umami goodness. This salad is vegan, using nutritional yeast to flavor the crackers and the dressing, and soft tofu in place of mayonnaise. If you are not vegan or do not have these elements on hand, feel free to use grated pecorino or Parmesan in place of the nutritional yeast, and mayonnaise in place of the silken tofu. And if you can't find fermented black beans, use a tablespoon or two of homemade (see page 143) or store-bought black bean sauce.

SERVES 4

VEGAN

Wonton–scallion crackers

10–15 wonton wrappers, halved into rectangles
2 tablespoons toasted sesame oil or extra-virgin olive oil
1 scallion, finely chopped
1–2 tablespoons nutritional yeast
Sea salt and black pepper

Black bean Caesar dressing

2 tablespoons fermented black beans, soaked in warm water for 10 minutes
10½ ounces (300 g) silken tofu
2 tablespoons nutritional yeast
1 garlic clove, finely chopped
1 tablespoon toasted white sesame seeds
1 tablespoon extra-virgin olive oil
1 tablespoon toasted sesame oil
Juice of ½ lime
1 scallion, finely chopped
Black pepper

1 napa (Chinese) cabbage, cut lengthwise into 6–8 wedges, with stem intact
Extra-virgin olive oil
1 scallion, finely sliced
Lime wedges
Sea salt and black pepper

Preheat the oven to 400°F (200°C) and line a large sheet pan with parchment paper.

For the wonton–scallion crackers, brush both sides of the wonton rectangles with oil and lay them out in a single layer on the prepared sheet pan. Sprinkle with the scallion and nutritional yeast, and season with a little sea salt and black pepper. Bake for 4–6 minutes or until the crackers are golden and crispy. Remove and cool, then break them into slightly smaller pieces.

Meanwhile, for the black bean Caesar dressing, drain the fermented black beans in a colander and rinse under cold running water. Drain well. Place the black beans, tofu, nutritional yeast, garlic, sesame seeds, olive oil, sesame oil and lime juice in a blender or food processor and whiz until smooth. Season with black pepper and stir in the scallion.

Heat a barbecue or grill pan over high heat. Drizzle each side of the cabbage wedges with olive oil. Place them cut-side down on the barbecue or in the grill pan and cook for 1–2 minutes, just long enough to achieve nice char marks.

Place the cabbage on a serving plate and season with sea salt and black pepper. Spoon over some of the black bean dressing and scatter with the wonton crackers and scallion. Serve immediately with lime wedges on the side.

Note: The wonton crackers can be kept in an airtight container for 3–4 days. For a heartier meal, add roasted chickpeas (see page 181).

Substitute

Fermented black beans: chopped marinated black olives, black bean sauce (store-bought or homemade, see page 143)
Silken tofu: good-quality mayonnaise
Nutritional yeast: grated pecorino or Parmesan

Maple-buttered sweet potato with lentils

Nishiki Market is known to locals as "Kyoto's pantry" for a reason—it's a mecca for traditional foods, with a staggering choice of tsukemono (Japanese pickles), yuba (tofu skin), wagashi (Japanese sweets), tako tamago (small skewered baby octopus with a quail's egg inside the head), deep-fried fish cakes, miso and tofu that is so fresh, it needs to be eaten on the spot. I fell in love with the grilled golden-fleshed sweet potato, which scorched our tongues as we devoured it straight from the coals. During the cooler months, yakiimo (roasted sweet potato) is, understandably, a popular street snack in Japan.

For this recipe, I recommend using Japanese sweet potatoes with their deep magenta skin and golden flesh—they are drier and creamier than orange sweet potatoes. The skin gets crispy and burnished after roasting, while the center becomes tender and pudding-like. The maple-accented butter is simple, rich and delicious, melting and becoming one with the sticky flesh. Purple Okinawan sweet potato is less sweet, but also a nice variety to use for this salad. And if you only have orange sweet potatoes, that's fine too.

SERVES 4–6
GLUTEN FREE

4–6 Japanese purple sweet potatoes (about 3⅓ pounds / 1.5 kg)
Extra-virgin olive oil
1 cup (200 g) Puy lentils
1 garlic clove, smashed
7 tablespoons (100 g) unsalted butter, at room temperature
2 tablespoons maple syrup
2 scallions, finely sliced
Sea salt and black pepper

Preheat the oven to 425°F (220°C).

Prick the sweet potatoes all over with a fork and place on a sheet pan. Drizzle with olive oil and sprinkle with sea salt, then bake for 45–60 minutes until the potatoes are very soft when squeezed.

Bring a saucepan of salted water to the boil over high heat and add the lentils and garlic. Reduce the heat to medium–low, then cover and cook for about 20 minutes until the lentils are just tender. Drain. Mash the garlic and fold it through the lentils, then dress with a little oil.

Meanwhile, mix together the butter, maple syrup and half the scallions. Season with a little sea salt.

Spoon the lentils onto a serving platter or arrange on individual plates. While the potatoes are still hot, cut a slit lengthwise down the middle and push in the sides to puff up the soft inner flesh. Place the sweet potatoes on top of the lentils and dollop generously with maple butter, allowing it to melt all over the potatoes and spill onto the lentils. Scatter with the remaining scallions, season with sea salt and black pepper, and serve immediately.

Note: The maple butter can be made in advance and kept in the fridge for 3–4 days. Remember to bring it to room temperature before using.

Substitute

Maple syrup: honey
Japanese purple sweet potato: regular orange sweet potato or Okinawan sweet potato

Veganize

Use vegan butter

Seaweed lettuce salad

SERVES 2–4
VEGAN AND GLUTEN-FREE

5 x 9-inch (12.5 x 22.5 cm) piece of kelp (kombu) (about ¾ ounce / 21 g), soaked in warm water for 15–20 minutes

1 head of lettuce (red oak or butter), leaves separated, washed and dried thoroughly

1 avocado, sliced or cut into thin wedges

1 tablespoon toasted white sesame seeds

1 scallion, finely chopped

Sea salt and black pepper

Spicy sesame dressing

1 garlic clove, grated

1 scallion, finely chopped

1 teaspoon sugar

1 tablespoon rice vinegar

1 tablespoon gochugaru (Korean red chile flakes) or 1 teaspoon red chile flakes

2 tablespoons toasted sesame oil

1 tablespoon toasted white sesame seeds

1 teaspoon sea salt

Seaweed is the vegetable I'm trying to incorporate more of into our family diet. It's not an obvious everyday food, but it should be. Seaweed is one of the world's most nutrient-rich and sustainable foods (for more, see my notes about seaweed on page 22). This salad is an easy and delicious way to add a little more seaweed to your diet, paired with fresh, crispy greens and a punchy sesame dressing.
I like to use kelp (kombu) in this salad, but it's also good with wakame or hijiki. Dried seaweed can be found at many supermarkets, health-food stores, Asian grocers or online.

Bring a saucepan of salted water to the boil, add the seaweed and boil for 12–15 minutes until tender-crisp. Drain. When cool enough to handle, tear or slice the kelp into bite-sized pieces.

For the spicy sesame dressing, mix together all the ingredients in a small bowl.

Combine the seaweed, lettuce and avocado in a bowl and pour over the dressing. Season with sea salt and black pepper, top with the sesame seeds and scallion and serve immediately.

Substitute

Kelp: other dried seaweed such as wakame, dulse or hijiki (rinse this type of seaweed well)

Dumpling salad

On days when I am really craving dumplings for dinner, but feel like I should opt for something greener, lighter and healthier, a dumpling salad is my perfect compromise. This is not really a recipe, but rather an idea—serve your favorite homemade or store-bought dumplings on a bed of salad leaves, add some fresh herbs and drizzle with a simple dipping sauce. There are so many options for the dressing— here, I have suggested the very reliable dumpling dipping sauce on page 29, but you could also drizzle over everything oil (page 25), ginger–scallion oil (page 28), spicy sesame dressing (page 189), black bean Caesar dressing (page 185), goma sauce (page 203), cilantro and lemongrass pesto (page 211) or your favorite vinaigrette.

SERVES 4–6
VEGAN (IF USING VEGAN DUMPLINGS)

20–25 of your favorite dumplings (see pages 118–127 for a range of dumpling recipes)

4 big handfuls of salad leaves, baby spinach or microgreens

2 Persian cucumbers, trimmed and very finely sliced

9 ounces (255 g) cherry tomatoes, halved

Handful of cilantro leaves

1 scallion, finely sliced

1 long red or green chile, seeds removed and finely sliced

Reliable Dumpling Dipping Sauce (see page 29)

Sea salt and black pepper

Prepare the dumplings by steaming or pan-frying them (see page 117 for cooking instructions).

Arrange the salad leaves on a large serving plate or platter. Place the warm dumplings on top and scatter over the cucumber, tomato, cilantro leaves, scallion and chile. Season with sea salt and black pepper, drizzle with your chosen dressing or sauce and serve immediately.

Whole roasted gochujang cauliflower with smashed roasted butter beans

SERVES 2–4

1–2 tablespoons gochujang (Korean fermented hot pepper paste)

½ cup (125 g) plain yogurt

Extra-virgin olive oil

1 large cauliflower (about 2¼ pounds / 1 kg)

1 lemon, halved

Handful of chopped parsley leaves

Handful of cilantro leaves

2 tablespoons flaked or slivered almonds, toasted

Sea salt and black pepper

Smashed roasted butter beans

1 pound (450 g) cooked butter beans (about two 14-ounce / 400-g cans, drained)

Extra-virgin olive oil

1 garlic clove, finely grated

1 teaspoon ground cumin

1 teaspoon ground coriander

½ teaspoon ground ginger

Sea salt and black pepper

Substitute

Cauliflower: whole cabbage

Butter beans: chickpeas, cannellini beans or lentils

Veganize

Use coconut or dairy-free yogurt

Whole roasted cauliflower is my go-to celebratory dish. It is a perfect canvas for all sorts of flavors and an impressive addition to a feasting table. Often, I roast a whole cauliflower purely for simplicity—I just massage it with olive oil, season with salt and pepper and leave it to roast, unhindered, for an hour.

This recipe is both a showstopper and an easy everyday dish. The whole cauliflower is bathed in a spicy and vibrantly hued gochujang-laced yogurt. Gochujang is both sweet and fiery, and while the yogurt will marginally tame this heat, I encourage you to add as little or as much as you like to the yogurt marinade, to suit your preferred spice levels. Mashing and smashing the butter beans a little before you roast them is a great way to create more surface area, resulting in maximum crispiness. You could also serve the cauliflower with a mound of rice, for an even heartier meal.

Preheat the oven to 425°F (220°C).

In a small bowl, whisk together the gochujang and yogurt and add a drizzle of oil.

Remove the outer leaves from the cauliflower and trim the stem so it is flush with the bottom of the cauliflower. Place the cauliflower on a sheet pan, drizzle with oil and season well with sea salt and black pepper. Place in the oven and roast for 45–50 minutes until the cauliflower is golden and just about cooked. Remove from the oven, drizzle with more oil and squeeze over the juice of ½ lemon. Massage about 2 tablespoons of the gochujang yogurt all over the cauliflower. Return to the oven and roast for another 10–15 minutes until completely tender (the exact cooking time will depend on the size of the cauliflower so check it often).

Meanwhile, for the smashed roasted butter beans, place the butter beans in a bowl and roughly mash with the back of a fork or a potato masher. You only need to break up some of the beans, not all of them, so the consistency is chunky. Add a good drizzle of oil, along with the garlic and cumin, ground coriander and ginger, then season with sea salt and black pepper and stir to combine. Place the butter beans on a separate sheet pan and roast for 20–30 minutes until crispy and golden.

To serve, spoon the smashed butter beans onto a large serving plate and place the roasted cauliflower on top. Dollop with the remaining gochujang yogurt, drizzle with some oil and season with sea salt and black pepper. Finish with the parsley, cilantro leaves and almonds and serve with the remaining lemon on the side.

Sweet potato with black-eyed peas and coconut vinaigrette

The aroma of black-eyed peas cooking on the stove is emphatically nostalgic for me, a scent that reminds me of my mother's jook (congee) or her nightly tong (soup). Black-eyed peas are full of nutrition, loaded with calcium, folate and protein, and in traditional Chinese medicine they are believed to aid digestion and nourish the kidney and spleen. Apart from the health benefits, I love the complex flavor of black-eyed peas, particularly in salads. In this dish, they are roasted alongside sweet potatoes until they're a little crispy, and then finished with a charming coconut vinaigrette. The vinaigrette is inspired by a salad I ate a few years ago at Kismet in Los Angeles—it was such a surprising dressing I couldn't get it out of my head. I was so infatuated that I had to create my own version.

SERVES 4
VEGAN AND GLUTEN FREE

10½ ounces (300 g) cooked black-eyed peas (about one 14-ounce / 400-g can, drained)

Extra-virgin olive oil

1 garlic clove, finely chopped

Zest of ½ lemon

6 sweet potatoes (about 3⅓ pounds / 1.5 kg), peeled and cut into ½-inch-thick (1.25 cm) discs

2 scallions, finely sliced

Big handful of cilantro leaves

Sea salt and black pepper

Coconut vinaigrette

⅓ cup (80 ml) coconut milk

1 tablespoon extra-virgin olive oil

1 tablespoon lemon juice

2 teaspoons brown sugar

1 teaspoon sea salt

Preheat the oven to 400°F (200°C).

Place the black-eyed peas in a bowl and drizzle with olive oil. Add the garlic and lemon zest, season with sea salt and black pepper and toss to coat.

Place the sweet potatoes in a single layer on a large sheet pan, drizzle with oil and season with sea salt and black pepper. Roast for 15 minutes. Add the black-eyed peas to the sheet pan and shake to mix everything up, then return to the oven for another 10–15 minutes, until the sweet potatoes are tender and the black-eyed peas are a little crispy.

Meanwhile, to make the vinaigrette, whisk together all the ingredients until smooth.

To serve, place the sweet potatoes and black-eyed peas on a serving plate and drizzle over the vinaigrette. Finish with a final drizzle of oil, season with sea salt and black pepper and scatter over the scallions and cilantro leaves.

Substitute

Black-eyed peas: chickpeas, cannellini beans or brown lentils

Sweet potato: butternut squash or cauliflower

Pad thai salad with shredded cabbage and kale

SERVES 4
VEGAN

Leaves from ½ bunch of kale
(about 120 g), finely sliced

½ small green or purple cabbage
(about 9 ounces / 255 g), finely sliced

1 lime, halved

12 ounces (350 g) wide rice noodles

Extra-virgin olive oil

3 radishes, finely sliced

2 scallions, finely sliced

20 basil leaves

Handful of cilantro leaves

3 tablespoons roasted peanuts,
roughly chopped

Sea salt and black pepper

Pad thai dressing

3 tablespoons brown sugar

3 tablespoons Vegan "Fish Sauce"
(see page 29)

1 tablespoon rice vinegar

1 tablespoon tamarind purée

1 tablespoon toasted sesame oil

¼ teaspoon red chile flakes

1 small garlic clove, finely chopped

Extra-virgin olive oil

Sea salt and black pepper

Substitute

Vegan "Fish Sauce": regular fish sauce

Kale: chard, shaved broccoli
or cauliflower

Cabbage: napa (Chinese) cabbage or
finely shaved Brussels sprouts

This is a fresher, crunchier version of crowd favorite, pad thai noodles. Rather than using cooked vegetables, I've used raw kale and cabbage, which I've softened by massaging in salt and lime. This leaves the veggies citrusy, with a bit of crunch, adding an exciting brightness to this classic noodle dish. You could use other veggies too—carrots would be a nice addition—and add pan-fried tofu slices if you want to increase the protein. The signature tamarind and lime flavors of pad thai are featured in the zesty dressing, while roasted chopped peanuts make a lovely textural topping.

To prepare the pad thai dressing, combine the brown sugar, fish sauce, rice vinegar, tamarind, sesame oil, chile flakes and garlic in a small saucepan over low heat and cook until the sugar has dissolved, about 1 minute. Remove from the heat. Add 1–2 tablespoons of olive oil and season with sea salt and black pepper.

Place the kale and cabbage in a large bowl, sprinkle with 1 teaspoon of sea salt and squeeze over the juice of ½ lime. Massage the salt and juice into the leaves to tenderize them, then leave to sit for 10 minutes.

Bring a large saucepan of salted water to the boil and cook the noodles according to the packet instructions, usually about 6–7 minutes. Rinse under cold running water and leave to drain.

To serve, combine the noodles, massaged leaves and dressing in a large bowl and toss to coat. Taste and season with sea salt and black pepper. Add the radish, scallions, basil and cilantro and toss gently. Transfer to a serving bowl and top with the peanuts, then serve with the remaining lime, cut into wedges, on the side.

Bibimbap salad bowl

SERVES 4–6
GLUTEN FREE

Vegetable or other neutral oil

14 ounces (400 g) extra-firm tofu, cut into ⅛-inch-thick (4 mm) slices

Extra-virgin olive oil

5½ ounces (155 g) fresh shiitake mushrooms, sliced

Leaves from ½ bunch of kale (about 4½ ounces / 125 g)

1 garlic clove, finely chopped

2–3 teaspoons toasted sesame oil

5½ ounces (155 g) bean sprouts

4 heaped cups (about 28 ounces / 800 g) cooled cooked rice

4–6 large eggs

3–4 teaspoons toasted white sesame seeds

3 tablespoons gochujang (Korean fermented hot pepper paste), diluted with 1 tablespoon of water

Sea salt and black pepper

Substitute

Kale: spinach or chard

Shiitake: oyster, cremini or button mushrooms

Veganize

Omit the egg

Bibimbap is the ultimate "leftovers" dish. My Korean friends tell me that it is often served as a way of eating up the days-old banchan (vegetable side dishes). Honestly, I can't think of a better way to use up leftovers or stray cuts of vegetables languishing in the crisper drawer. My bibimbap salad bowls feature crispy rice topped with tofu, mushrooms, kale and bean sprouts, however you can use whatever vegetables you have on hand. There are a number of steps, but they are all very simple. For a dinner party, serve the crispy rice alongside bowls of vegetables in the center of the table, and allow guests to build their own bowls. The fried egg is optional, of course.

Heat a drizzle of oil in a large frying pan over medium–high heat, add the tofu slices in a single layer and season well with sea salt and black pepper. Cook for 2–3 minutes until golden, then flip the slices over and repeat on the other side. Remove from the pan and set aside to cool, then slice the tofu into triangles or rectangles. Wipe out the pan with paper towels (do this after you cook each ingredient).

In the same pan over medium heat, add another drizzle of oil. When hot, add the shiitake mushrooms and season with sea salt and black pepper. Cook for 2–3 minutes, turning, until the mushrooms are golden. Remove and set aside.

Heat another drizzle of oil in the pan, then add the kale and garlic and season with sea salt and black pepper. Cook for 2–3 minutes until wilted. Remove from the pan and drizzle with a little of the sesame oil. Set aside.

Return the pan to medium heat and add a little more oil. Toss in the bean sprouts and cook for 1 minute until they are slightly wilted. Remove from the pan and drain. Place the sprouts in a small bowl, drizzle with the remaining sesame oil and season with sea salt and black pepper. Set aside.

Add a good drizzle of oil to the pan and place over medium–low heat. Add the rice, season with sea salt and turn it in the oil for 1 minute. Flatten it down into the pan with a wooden spoon or spatula and cook, undisturbed, for 5–7 minutes until the rice is golden and crispy on the bottom. Flip over the rice (if the pan is dry, drizzle in some more oil) and leave to cook undisturbed for another 4–5 minutes until the rice is brown on both sides.

Meanwhile, place another frying pan over medium–high heat and add a drizzle of oil. Fry each egg until the whites are set but the yolks are still runny.

Divide the crispy rice among serving bowls and top with the tofu, mushrooms, kale, bean sprouts, sesame seeds and a fried egg. Drizzle over the gochujang sauce and season with a little sea salt.

Pasta salad with umeboshi vinaigrette

Considered a Japanese superfood, umeboshi are salted Japanese plums or apricots. They have been used medicinally in China and Japan for more than 3,000 years, to cure anything from hangovers to indigestion and upset tummies. Small plums or apricots are pickled, covered in salt and left to ferment (red shiso leaves are added to dye the umeboshi their signature shade of pink). The result is a flavor-rich vegan umami bomb, adding an intensely fruity saltiness to food, similar to preserved lemon, fish sauce or Parmesan. I fell in love with pickled plums while in Tokyo, where I devoured an umeboshi onigiri for breakfast every morning, and it has been a constant in my pantry ever since. Although the flavor is strong, when it is used in cooking it adds a mellow yet confident punch to the meal. You could also add umeboshi to pesto, soup, risotto, Caesar dressing, pasta sauce or stew. It is particularly compelling in this pasta salad, delivering a salty, sour and fragrant richness that makes this dish sing.

A note about umeboshi—I usually buy the jars of round plums with seeds inside, but it is sometimes sold as a paste, which works well too. I usually buy mine from a Japanese or Asian grocer, or health-food store. You can also find umeboshi plums and paste online.

SERVES 4–6
VEGAN

1 pound (450 g) small pasta shapes

Olive oil

5½ ounces (155 g) green beans, trimmed

3½ ounces (100 g) kale leaves, finely shredded

3 tablespoons toasted sunflower seeds

1 long red chile, finely chopped (remove the seeds if you prefer less heat)

2 scallions, finely sliced

Handful of cilantro leaves

1 lime, halved

Sea salt and black pepper

Umeboshi vinaigrette

5 umeboshi (about 2 ounces / 60 g)

1 garlic clove, grated

⅓ cup (80 ml) extra-virgin olive oil

1 teaspoon toasted sesame oil

Sea salt and black pepper

Bring a large saucepan of salted water to the boil, add the pasta and cook according to the packet instructions until al dente, about 8–12 minutes. Drain and refresh under cold running water.

Heat a frying pan over medium–high heat. When hot, add a drizzle of olive oil, toss in the green beans and season with sea salt. Cook for 2–3 minutes, until slightly charred and just tender. Remove from the pan and roughly chop.

To make the vinaigrette, remove the seeds from the umeboshi and chop the flesh until it resembles a paste. Whisk it together with the garlic, oils and 3 tablespoons of water until well combined. Taste and season with a little sea salt and black pepper.

Combine the pasta, green beans, kale, sunflower seeds, chile, scallions and cilantro leaves in a large bowl. Pour over the umeboshi vinaigrette and squeeze in the lime juice. Toss, taste and season with sea salt and black pepper.

Substitute

Umeboshi: miso, preserved lemon or Chinese fermented bean curd

Green beans: broccoli

Kale: baby spinach or arugula

Sunflower seeds: sesame seeds, pumpkin seeds or almonds

Use gluten-free pasta for gluten free

Green bean goma-ae and chilled soba noodle salad

SERVES 4
VEGAN

10 ounces (280 g) soba noodles

Extra-virgin olive oil or toasted sesame oil

10½ ounces (300 g) green beans, trimmed

4 scallions, finely sliced

Sea salt and black pepper

Goma (sesame) sauce

⅓ cup (50 g) toasted white sesame seeds

⅓ cup (80 ml) tamari or soy sauce

2 tablespoons sugar

2 teaspoons mirin

2 teaspoons rice vinegar

Goma-ae is a classic Japanese side dish of blanched vegetables with sesame dressing. The sesame sauce is perfectly balanced—sweet and salty, with the right amount of umami—and should instantly go into your repertoire of easy Asian-style dressings for veggies and noodles. In Japanese cuisine, blanched spinach is also commonly served with this sesame sauce, but you could sub in almost any blanched vegetable—broccoli and asparagus also work nicely. This green bean goma-ae also goes well with rice.

Bring a large saucepan of salted water to the boil, add the soba noodles and cook according to the packet instructions until just tender, about 3–5 minutes. Drain immediately and refresh under cold running water. Drain again, drizzle with some oil (to prevent sticking) and toss. Place in the fridge to chill while you prepare the rest of the salad.

To make the goma sauce, place the sesame seeds in a mortar and grind with a pestle until mostly broken up; leave some seeds unground for texture. Add the remaining ingredients and mix together to form a paste. Set aside.

Bring a large saucepan of salted water to the boil, add the green beans and cook for 2–3 minutes, until they are bright green and just tender. Drain immediately and refresh under cold running water. Drain well to remove as much excess water as you can.

Place the green beans in a bowl, add the goma sauce and stir to coat the beans. Add the soba noodles, along with a drizzle of oil, season with sea salt and black pepper and toss everything together. Scatter with the scallions and serve immediately, or chill in the fridge for up to 4 hours until you are ready to eat.

Note: Soba noodles are best served chilled in salads. You can prepare the noodles 1–2 days ahead, then dress in a little oil to prevent them from sticking and keep in the fridge until you are ready to use them.

Substitute

Green beans: spinach, broccoli, asparagus or carrot

Soba noodles: udon, rice or ramen noodles

White sesame seeds: black sesame seeds

Use gluten-free noodles and gluten-free soy sauce for gluten free

A green salad, with kumquats

SERVES 4
VEGAN AND GLUTEN FREE

4 large handfuls of salad leaves

2 Persian cucumbers, finely sliced into discs

1 pound (450 g) cooked chickpeas (about two 14-ounce / 400-g cans, drained)

6–8 kumquats, very finely sliced

Handful of cilantro leaves

Extra-virgin olive oil

Sea salt and black pepper

Herby tahini

1 cup (20 g) soft herbs (I like a combination of cilantro, parsley, mint and basil leaves)

⅓ cup (90 g) tahini

1 garlic clove, grated

Juice of ½ lemon, plus extra if needed

Sea salt and black pepper

Substitute

Chickpeas: white beans or butter beans

Kumquats: preserved lemon, orange or lemon zest

My mother has several kumquat trees in her garden. The kumquat tree in the backyard grows oval-shaped fruit with thin skin, so sour that we wince as we bite into them. Each year, the tree bears an abundant bounty of zingy fruit, which my mother dutifully turns into pickles or liqueur. There is a second kumquat tree at the front of the house, which tastes of gold. Thick skinned and sugary, with a mellow flesh inside, I eat these juicy fruit right off the branch. My love of kumquats, both sour and sweet, inspired this salad, an adaptable everyday green salad with a bit of extra love from fresh kumquats and an earthy herby tahini. If you can't find kumquats, you can go without, or perhaps add another punchy citrus like preserved lemon.

To make the herby tahini, place the herbs, tahini, garlic and lemon juice in a blender or food processor, along with about 3 tablespoons of water (add a tablespoon at a time, adding more water if necessary) and blend until smooth. Taste and add more lemon juice, if needed. Season with sea salt and black pepper. (If you don't have a food processor or blender, you can finely chop the herbs with a knife, then whisk in a bowl with the remaining ingredients.)

To assemble the salad, place the salad leaves on one or two large plates. Top with the cucumber, scatter over the chickpeas and dollop over the herby tahini. Dot with the kumquats and cilantro leaves and finish with a drizzle of olive oil. Season with sea salt and black pepper and serve immediately.

Nashi pears with bitter leaves and goat's cheese

SERVES 2–4
GLUTEN FREE

2 large nashi pears, cored and peeled

Extra-virgin olive oil

2 handfuls of baby arugula or spinach leaves (or a combination)

1 endive or small radicchio, trimmed and leaves separated

2 ounces (60 g) goat's cheese, crumbled

1 scallion, finely sliced

Sea salt and black pepper

Shallot–lemon vinaigrette

1 shallot, finely chopped

Zest and juice of ½ lemon (about 2 tablespoons juice), plus extra if needed

2–3 tablespoons extra-virgin olive oil

1 teaspoon Dijon mustard

1 teaspoon maple syrup

1 small garlic clove, finely grated

Sea salt and black pepper

My mother would often present meticulously segmented nashi pears as an afternoon snack. While not your everyday fruit, nashi pears (also known as Asian/Chinese/Korean pears) have actually been grown for thousands of years in Asia, and are particularly significant in Japan, where they were one of the very first crops to be cultivated. Here, I pan-fry nashi pears until just golden (don't overcook them or they'll get mushy) and toss them with mildly bitter leaves and tangy goat's cheese. The shallot–lemon vinaigrette is an elegant dressing, and one that I often use for a plain leafy green salad.

Cut each pear into 12–16 wedges, depending on the size of your fruit. Heat a frying pan over high heat and drizzle with oil. Working in batches, place the pear wedges in the pan in a single layer and cook for about 2 minutes on each side, until golden and tender-crisp. Remove and set aside.

For the shallot–lemon vinaigrette, whisk together the shallot, lemon zest and juice and 1 tablespoon of water in a bowl. Slowly whisk in the oil, then add the mustard, maple syrup and garlic and season well with sea salt and black pepper. Taste and add more salt and lemon, if needed.

To assemble, place the salad leaves and endive or radicchio on a large plate, top with the pear wedges and scatter with goat's cheese. Drizzle over the vinaigrette and season with sea salt and black pepper. Gently toss together, then finish with a scattering of scallion and serve.

Substitute

Nashi pear: Bosc or Bartlett pear

Goat's cheese: ricotta or blue cheese

Maple syrup: honey

Veganize

Omit the goat's cheese

Roasted roots with chile–oat crisp

Eating a Chinese meal with chile sauce on the side is a muscle memory for my taste buds, and a fundamental part of the experience. In Asian culture, the type of chile sauce you apply can really change the character of a dish. This chile–oat crisp is similar to my everything oil (see page 25) in that it is a stand-alone sauce. Drizzling it on noodles instantly makes it a meal. At Asian grocers, you can find a product called Lao Gan Ma Spicy Chili Crisp, hailing from China's Guizhou province. This garlicky, spicy, crunchy condiment is served with everything from noodles to ice cream to peanut brittle. The defining characteristic of this chile sauce is the crispness, and in my version I've included old-fashioned rolled oats and coconut flakes for extra crunch. You will find me adding it to pasta, eggs, jook, pizza and, of course, roasted vegetables. Here, I team roasted root vegetables with mung beans, and use the chile–oat crisp as a simple dressing. Vary the amount of spice in your chile crisp according to your tastes.

SERVES 4
VEGAN

2¼ pounds (1 kg) your favorite root vegetables (I use carrots, sweet potatoes, potatoes, turnips and beets)

Extra-virgin olive oil

1 leek, white and pale green parts only, finely sliced

½ cup (100 g) mung beans

1 small garlic clove, peeled

2 scallions, finely sliced

⅓ cup (50 g) roasted peanuts, chopped

Sea salt and black pepper

Chile–oat crisp

3 shallots, finely diced

2 garlic cloves, finely chopped

1-inch (2.5 cm) piece of ginger, peeled and finely chopped

1 cinnamon stick

1 cup (100 g) old-fashioned rolled oats

½ cup (30 g) coconut flakes, roughly chopped

3 tablespoons toasted white sesame seeds

3 tablespoons red chile flakes

1½ cups (375 ml) vegetable or other neutral oil

2 tablespoons toasted sesame oil

About 1 tablespoon sea salt

Preheat the oven to 400°F (200°C).

Scrub the root vegetables (I don't usually peel them, but please do if you prefer) and cut them into 1-inch (2.5 cm) pieces. Place on a large sheet pan in a single layer, drizzle with olive oil and season with sea salt and black pepper. Roast for 15 minutes, then remove from the oven and add the leek to the sheet pan. Drizzle the leek with a little oil and roast for another 10–20 minutes or so, until everything is soft and golden. Set aside.

Meanwhile, bring a saucepan of salted water to the boil, add the mung beans and garlic and cook for 25–30 minutes, until tender. Drain and mash the very soft garlic into the beans.

To make the chile–oat crisp, place the shallots, garlic, ginger, cinnamon stick, oats, coconut flakes, sesame seeds, chile flakes and oils in a saucepan over medium heat. Bring to a gentle simmer, swirling the pan every now and then, then reduce the heat to medium–low and cook for 20–25 minutes until everything is crispy.

Strain the oil through a sieve over a bowl and leave the oat mixture to cool in the sieve—this will allow it to crisp up further. Set the oil aside. Once the crispy oat mixture is completely cool, stir it back into the oil and season with the sea salt. Leave the cinnamon stick in the oil, as it will continue to flavor it. Store the chile–oat crisp in a sterilized jar at room temperature. It will keep well for several months.

To serve, place the mung beans and vegetables on a serving plate, spoon over a few tablespoons of the chile–oat crisp (enough to suit the level of spice you prefer) and season with sea salt and black pepper. Scatter with the scallions and peanuts.

Substitute

Rolled oats: gluten-free oats for gluten free

Bright and lively potato salad with fennel, watercress and cilantro and lemongrass pesto

Not all potato salads are created equal. The potato salads of my childhood were made with commercial dressings, and were, to be blunt, rather bland. Ironically, salads were not my mum's strong suit—apart from her jellyfish and celery salad, which was a showstopper. Making "Western-style" salads to be served at backyard barbecues was her attempt to assimilate to the way she thought other Australian families entertained.

This recipe shows how exciting a potato salad can be when we embrace Asian flavors. It required a few descriptors in the title because it is so full of life and color—I chose "bright and lively," but it easily could have been "crisp and fresh," or perhaps "spicy and aromatic." The cilantro and lemongrass pesto is absolutely delicious and could also be served with pasta, noodles, a rice bowl or roasted veggies.

SERVES 4–6
VEGAN AND GLUTEN FREE

2¼ pounds (1 kg) red potatoes (or other waxy variety), peeled and cut into 1½-inch (3.75 cm) pieces

Extra-virgin olive oil

1 fennel bulb, finely shaved, fronds reserved

½ bunch of watercress (about 3½ ounces / 100 g), stems trimmed, leaves torn in half

1 lime, cut into wedges

Sea salt and black pepper

Cilantro and lemongrass pesto

1 bunch of cilantro (including the roots if they come with it), washed and roughly chopped

2 lemongrass stalks, white part only, roughly chopped

½–1 jalapeño chile, roughly chopped

2 garlic cloves, roughly chopped

1 tablespoon rice vinegar

1 tablespoon tamari or gluten-free soy sauce

⅓ cup (50 g) roasted cashews, roughly chopped

1 tablespoon toasted sesame oil

⅓ cup (80 ml) extra-virgin olive oil

Sea salt and black pepper

Substitute

Watercress: baby arugula leaves or other seasonal leaves like purslane

Jalapeño: serrano or long green chile

Preheat the oven to 400°F (200°C).

Spread out the potato on a sheet pan, then drizzle with olive oil and season with sea salt and black pepper. Roast for about 30 minutes, or until soft and golden. Turn off the heat but leave the potatoes in the oven to keep warm.

To make the pesto, place the cilantro, lemongrass, chile and garlic in a blender or food processor and blend until everything is broken up. Add the rice vinegar, tamari or soy sauce and cashews and, with the motor running, slowly trickle in both oils until it forms a chunky paste. If it's too thick, add 1 tablespoon of water. Season with sea salt and black pepper.

Place the warm potatoes in a large bowl and add the fennel, a few reserved fronds and the watercress. Add the pesto and gently toss to combine. Taste and, if needed, season with sea salt and black pepper. Finish with a good squeeze of lime juice and serve with extra wedges.

Spicy celery, tofu and glass noodle salad

The dish from my childhood that sparked my love for salad was my mother's spicy jellyfish salad. Long rubbery strands, tossed with slivers of celery and chicken, coated in a vinegary sesame sauce. It was a "special occasion" dish, one she would only serve at birthday parties and family gatherings. For much of my life as a salad maker, I have passionately sought to recreate the chewy, crispy, robust textures of this salad. While jellyfish free, this version is a strong nod to my mum's dish, showcasing the loveliness of celery and tofu smothered in a sesame–vinegar dressing that feels comforting and familiar. I love the springy texture of glass noodles but, for something different, you could also try kelp noodles, which are made of seaweed and retain a lovely chewiness when blanched.

Bring a large saucepan of salted water to the boil, add the noodles and cook according to the packet instructions until just tender, about 5–6 minutes. In the last 30 seconds of cooking, add the celery and Asian greens to blanch. Drain and refresh under cold running water, then, using kitchen scissors, randomly cut the noodles two or three times to make some of the strands shorter and easier to eat. Leave to drain well.

For the sesame–vinegar dressing, whisk together all the ingredients in a small bowl. Taste and season with a little more sea salt, if required.

Combine the noodles, celery, greens and tofu in a bowl. Pour over the dressing, season with sea salt and toss to coat the noodles. Top with the sesame seeds, scallions and cilantro leaves and serve.

SERVES 4–6
VEGAN AND GLUTEN FREE

12 ounces (350 g) glass noodles (also known as sweet potato noodles)

3 celery stalks (about 7 ounces / 200 g), finely sliced diagonally

5½ ounces (155 g) Asian greens, trimmed and halved

9 ounces (255 g) five-spice tofu or pan-fried tofu (see page 183), cut into thin strips

1 tablespoon toasted white sesame seeds

2 scallions, finely sliced

Handful of cilantro leaves

Sea salt

Sesame–vinegar dressing

⅓ cup (80 ml) rice vinegar

3 tablespoons tamari or gluten-free soy sauce

3 tablespoons toasted sesame oil

1 tablespoon sugar

2–3 teaspoons Everything Oil (see page 25), Rayu (see page 26) or other chile oil

1 tablespoon toasted white sesame seeds

Sea salt

Substitute

Glass noodles: kelp noodles, mung bean vermicelli or rice vermicelli

Asian greens: broccoli, kale or baby spinach

An ode to Chang's crispy noodle salad

There was a time in the early 2000s when Chang's Fried Noodle Salad, the recipe on the back of the Chang's Fried Noodles packet, was the dish to bring to a McKinnon family gathering. The salad brought harmony to the anarchy of potluck tables, an affable salad that was both sophisticated and daring. This salad always felt ahead of its time, upholding all the nuances essential to a great salad—sweetness and saltiness in the soy–sesame dressing, freshness in the raw cabbage, herbaceousness from the scallions and crunch from the fried noodles.

This is my take, featuring two types of cabbage and tofu for extra heartiness. Of course, if you can get them, use Chang's Original Fried Noodles (or any other fried noodles in a packet) for this salad. If not, make your own fried noodles using instant ramen noodles; see below for instructions.

To make the sesame dressing, whisk together all the ingredients in a small bowl.

Combine the tofu, cabbages, scallions and almonds in a large bowl, pour over the dressing and toss to combine. Taste and season with sea salt and black pepper. Add the noodles just before serving and finish with the sesame seeds. Eat immediately.

Note: For those who didn't grow up in Australia, Chang's Original Fried Noodles are ubiquitous packets of crispy fried noodles found in every supermarket—they are an Aussie institution.

To make your own crispy fried noodles, bring a saucepan of water to the boil and add 1 block of instant ramen noodles. Cook for about 30 seconds less than the time specified on the packet—you want the noodles to be al dente. Drain immediately and refresh under cold running water. Pat the noodles dry with paper towels or a clean tea towel and cut them roughly with scissors so the strands are shorter. Sprinkle with about 2 tablespoons of cornstarch or potato starch (to soak up any excess moisture). Pour about 1 inch (2.5 cm) of vegetable oil into a frying pan and heat over high heat. When hot, drop in a handful of noodles and fry until crisp and lightly golden, about 2–3 minutes. Remove immediately and drain on paper towels. Continue until all the noodles are fried. You can store them in an airtight container for up to 10 days.

SERVES 4–6
VEGAN

9 ounces (255 g) five-spice tofu or pan-fried tofu (see page 183), cut into thin strips

½ napa (Chinese) cabbage (about 1 pound / 450 g), finely sliced

¼ savoy or green cabbage (about 7 ounces / 200 g), finely sliced

8 scallions, finely sliced

1 cup (110 g) slivered almonds, toasted

3½ ounces (100 g) packet crispy fried noodles

2 tablespoons toasted white sesame seeds

Sea salt and black pepper

Sesame dressing

3 tablespoons apple cider vinegar

3 tablespoons sugar

1 tablespoon tamari or soy sauce

1 small garlic clove, grated

1 tablespoon toasted sesame oil

3 tablespoons extra-virgin olive oil

Sea salt and black pepper

Substitute

Use gluten-free fried noodles and gluten-free soy sauce for gluten free

Green papaya salad, but with apple

I would eat som tam (green papaya salad) every day if I could. With adroitly balanced sour, sweet, spicy and savory flavors, this version offers an unexpected twist, replacing hard-to-find green papaya with everyday Granny Smith apples. As it turns out, green apples are a more than worthy substitute—they add a hint of extra sweetness, but also tartness, and stand up assertively to the big flavors. The vegan "fish sauce" is a handy little recipe, delivering that hit of indefinable deliciousness that we expect from an umami ingredient. I usually make this salad using my super-sized mortar and pestle, where all the ingredients are tossed in and pressed together, but if you only have a small one, simply smash your ingredients in batches, then mix them all together to serve.

SERVES 4
VEGAN AND GLUTEN FREE

2 garlic cloves, peeled

½ cup (75 g) roasted peanuts, roughly chopped

3½ ounces (100 g) snake beans, trimmed and cut into 1-inch (2.5 cm) pieces

10 cherry tomatoes, halved

½ lime, cut into 4 wedges

1–2 bird's eye or long red chiles (or more if you like it spicy)

2 Granny Smith apples (about 1 pound / 450 g)

Handful of basil leaves, torn

Sea salt

Tamarind dressing

1 tablespoon tamarind purée

3 tablespoons brown sugar

2 tablespoons Vegan "Fish Sauce" (see page 29)

Pinch of sea salt

Using a mortar and pestle, smash the garlic along with a big pinch of sea salt, then add half the peanuts and pound together until you have a rough paste. Add the beans, tomatoes and lime wedges and pound until bruised and crushed. Finally, add the chiles and pound just a few times—the more you pound, the spicier the salad will be! Scoop everything out of the mortar and place in a large bowl.

Peel the apples and slice into very thin matchsticks. Place in the mortar, a handful at a time, and lightly bruise them with the pestle. Add the bruised apple to the peanut mixture.

For the tamarind dressing, whisk together all the ingredients until the sugar and salt have dissolved. Taste—it should be a balance of sour, salty and sweet. Adjust the seasonings if necessary.

Add the dressing and basil to the salad and toss to coat. Sprinkle with the remaining peanuts and serve.

Substitute

Granny Smith apples: tart red apples, green papaya or green mango

Snake beans: sugar snap peas or blanched green beans

Not too
sweet

Sweet, but just a bit

The cake is ceremoniously ornate, haughtily smothered in pearly white cream, topped with meticulously crafted fruit. As the cake is cut, and generous pieces are handed around, my aunt (my mother's younger sister) is usually first out of the gate. She takes a bite, looks at my mum, and declares emphatically, "it's nice, not too sweet." My mother takes her bite and agrees approvingly, "yes, not too sweet." We all smile, amused that the Asian "not too sweet" custom is alive and well in our family.

This ritual is guaranteed at every celebration where cake or sweets are served. It is also a Chinese person's highest praise for a dessert. In Chinese culture, sweetness is enjoyed, but always with restraint. The Chinese bakery cake described above is a classic "not too sweet" cake, a light and fluffy sponge layered with cream and fruit, enveloped in a heavy layer of stiff "cream" that tastes suspiciously like mock cream.

Asian sweets are often low on the sweet spectrum. When we were kids we didn't eat desserts regularly, and the ones we did enjoy were often a little savory or even bitter. My mother sometimes made grass jelly, slightly bitter black gelatinous cubes served with a caramelly rock sugar syrup. One of my favorite desserts was black sesame soup, a classic Cantonese tong sui (sweet soup) made of ground black sesame seeds, glutinous rice flour and rock sugar, with a flavor that was sweet but also earthy and a little savory. But the most common dessert in our home was fruit. My dad was obsessive about oranges; at home he finished every meal with a perfectly segmented orange. Accordingly, refreshing fruit and fruity desserts are still my favorite "not too sweet" way to complete a meal.

Lychee and ginger soft serve

As warm days trickled into mild evenings, my mother would call me out to our front porch, bowl of fresh lychees in hand. We sat side by side, the lychees between us, surveying our sober suburban street, silent save for the occasional click of the clandestine cicadas, the air thick with the sweet notes of blooming jasmine. We peeled, ate and compared the size of our seeds—the lucky one got the smaller seeds, of course. Sometimes she would take the bowl inside and refill it. She would tell me about her garden, and sometimes I would wander over to my favorite kumquat tree and pop a few golden nuggets straight into my mouth. Lychees on the porch, lychees from the can, lychees in boxes as family gifts at Christmas time. For me, lychees are sweet remembrance.

This lychee soft serve is inspired by those quiet, warm evenings of my youth. Resplendent with the unique citrusy-rose flavor of lychees, this is the simplest ice-cream recipe, whipped up in minutes thanks to the magic of sweetened condensed milk. After just one hour you will enjoy a supple soft serve; leave it longer for a firmer texture. For simplicity and accessibility, I use canned lychees, which are incredibly nostalgic, but fresh ones work too.

This recipe is very adaptable. You can use berries or mango in place of the lychees, or frozen fruit for instant soft serve.

SERVES 6–8
GLUTEN FREE

1 pound (450 g) lychees, drained if canned

1 (14-ounce / 396-g) can sweetened condensed milk

2 teaspoons ground ginger

1 teaspoon vanilla extract

Place all the ingredients in a high-speed blender or food processor and whiz until smooth. Pour the creamy mixture into a loaf pan that measures approximately 5 x 9 inches (12.5 x 22.5 cm), cover and freeze for at least 1 hour. Alternatively, freeze for up to 5 days and let stand at room temperature for 10 minutes (to soften a little) before serving.

Black sticky rice pudding with lime-pickled pineapple

SERVES 4
VEGAN AND GLUTEN FREE

1 cup (200 g) black sticky (sweet or glutinous) rice, soaked overnight

⅓ cup (20 g) coconut flakes

1 (13.5-ounce / 398 ml) can coconut milk, stirred well

½ cup (95 g) brown sugar

Sea salt

Lime-pickled pineapple

10½ ounces (300 g) peeled pineapple, cut into chunks

Juice of ½ lime

1 tablespoon brown sugar

¼ teaspoon ground cinnamon

Rice pudding is a universal comfort food, prevalent across many disparate cultures. From the cardamom- and coconut-laced basmati rice pudding known as kheer in India, to eggy Greek rizogalo, Portuguese sweet rice, Swedish rice pudding, Cuban arroz con leche and sticky Filipino biko, the pairing of rice and milk seems to be a common sweet language. Black sticky rice pudding is one of my favorite Asian desserts—a common street snack in Thailand and Indonesia, it is rich and nutty, with a distinct chewy texture. The hint of salt at the end of cooking is essential, bringing that lovely salty-sweet duality to the dish. I like to serve it with a refreshing lime-pickled pineapple, accented with cinnamon, but you can also enjoy it without fruit. Plan ahead by soaking the rice in water overnight, covered and at room temperature; if you forget to do this, you can soak it in hot water for 30–60 minutes to soften it before cooking.

Drain the black rice, then place it in a saucepan with 2 cups (500 ml) of water and a pinch of sea salt. Cover and bring to the boil, then reduce the heat to low and simmer covered for for 35–45 minutes, until the grains are just tender. If it becomes too dry, add a touch more water. Drain.

Meanwhile, to prepare the lime-pickled pineapple, place all the ingredients in a bowl and toss to combine. Set aside while the black rice cooks.

Place the coconut flakes in a small dry frying pan over medium–low heat and toast, moving them around constantly to prevent burning. As soon as they are a light golden color, take them straight off the heat.

Set aside 3 tablespoons of the coconut milk to use as a topping.

Return the drained rice to the pan and add the brown sugar and remaining coconut milk. Bring to the boil, then reduce the heat to low and simmer covered for 20–25 minutes until the rice is completely tender, but still chewy. Stir in ½ teaspoon of sea salt. Remove from the heat and allow to cool to room temperature.

Ladle the just-warm rice into bowls and top with the pickled pineapple and a drizzle of the reserved coconut milk. Top with the toasted coconut flakes and serve. This black sticky rice pudding can also be served chilled.

Substitute

Pineapple: mango or lychees

Mango pudding

As a child, my version of a candy store was the desserts trolley at dim sum. While I didn't have a sweet tooth, it just felt magical to see the artistically crafted sweets being wheeled from table to table. I always wanted to be the one pushing the trolley—I imagined myself a skilled server-slash-salesperson, confidently dishing out plates of multi-colored jelly cubes decorated with little toothpick flags, wobbly black sesame rolls, glutinous rice balls (mochi) blanketed in coconut and, of course, egg tarts.

Mango pudding is another star of the dessert trolley, luminously orange, topped with evaporated milk and light as a feather to eat. This recipe is vegan, using agar agar powder (a jelly-like substance obtained from red algae) to achieve the gelatinous consistency. You'll find agar agar at specialty grocers or health-food stores.

SERVES 4
VEGAN AND GLUTEN FREE

1 pound (450 g) cubed mango (from about 3 ripe mangoes), plus 1 extra mango

1 (13.5-ounce / 398 ml) can coconut milk

⅓ cup (80 ml) maple syrup

1 teaspoon agar agar powder

Set aside one-quarter of the cubed mango and 3 tablespoons of the coconut milk.

Place the remaining cubed mango, remaining coconut milk and maple syrup in a blender or food processor and blend until completely smooth.

Pour the blitzed mango into a saucepan and whisk in the agar agar powder. Place over medium heat and bring to a gentle simmer, whisking constantly, until the agar agar has dissolved and the mixture has thickened. This should take about 5–7 minutes.

Cut the extra mango into slightly smaller cubes and divide among four bowls. Pour the mango and coconut mixture over the top and place in the fridge for 2 hours to set. Just before serving, top with the reserved mango cubes and drizzle with the reserved coconut milk.

Tamarind apple crisp

SERVES 6
GLUTEN FREE

Apple and tamarind filling

½ cup (95 g) brown sugar

2 tablespoons cornstarch

1 teaspoon ground cinnamon

2¼ pounds (1 kg) apples (such as Granny Smith or pink lady), peeled, cored and cut into ¼-inch-thick (6 mm) slices

⅓ cup (90 g) tamarind purée

1 teaspoon vanilla extract

Crisp topping

2 cups (200 g) gluten-free rolled oats

½ cup (95 g) brown sugar

½ teaspoon sea salt

1 stick (8 tablespoons / 115 g) unsalted butter, melted and cooled

3 tablespoons slivered or flaked almonds

Vanilla ice cream or whipped cream, to serve

Substitute

Tamarind purée: lemon juice or white (shiro) miso paste

Apple: pears or nashi pears

Cornstarch: potato or tapioca starch

Veganize

Use vegan butter in the topping and serve with vegan ice cream

This is a fun twist on a fruit crisp, a classic apple filling laced with sweet-sour tamarind—an unexpected yet delightful pairing. While the tamarind is subtle, it adds a hint of tartness, amplifies the apple flavor, and imparts a deep caramelized note. If you can't find tamarind, you could change the flavor profile slightly by replacing it with miso paste—you'd only need 1–2 tablespoons to add a rich umami note to the apples.

This crisp topping is a gift—I often make extra and keep batches in the freezer, which means that as long as I have fresh fruit on hand, I can throw together a dessert almost instantly. In the summer, I enjoy peach and blueberry crisp; in the spring, rhubarb and strawberry is my favorite; and in autumn, I opt for pear with a hint of ginger. This crisp recipe is also gluten free, making it an excellent stand-by dessert for unexpected guests.

Preheat the oven to 350°F (180°C). Spray a 9-inch (22.5 cm) round pie dish with cooking oil (or grease with butter).

For the apple and tamarind filling, combine the brown sugar, cornstarch and cinnamon in a bowl, whisking to remove any lumps. Add the apple, tamarind purée and vanilla extract and toss to coat. Transfer to the prepared dish and spread into a single, even layer.

To make the topping, pour half the rolled oats into a blender or food processor and blitz until it resembles flour. Transfer to a bowl, add the remaining whole rolled oats, brown sugar, sea salt, butter and almonds and stir to combine.

Scatter the topping over the apple mixture, leaving some large clumps intact. Bake for 50–60 minutes until the apple filling is juicy and bubbling around the edge of the dish, and the topping is golden. Remove and leave to cool for 15-20 minutes to allow the fruit to set.

Serve in bowls, with vanilla ice cream or whipped cream.

Note: The topping can be made in advance and stored in the fridge for up to 3 days or in the freezer for 3 months. The cooled crisp can be kept in the fridge for up to 1 week; gently reheat in a low oven for 20 minutes or enjoy cold or at room temperature.

Banana and black sesame loaf

Growing up, bananas were ever-present in my life. My father worked at Flemington Markets in Sydney where he traded in bananas, and a perk of his job was that our house was always brimming with bundles of this golden fruit. This overabundance meant that we generally didn't eat a lot of them; we gifted them to family, friends, neighbors and anybody who would take them. Jaded by bananas, I preferred to gorge on stone fruit, mangoes and melons. As I got older, and was no longer surrounded by mounds of bananas on the dining table, or in boxes in the laundry, they became a source of sweet memories and bittersweet nostalgia. I found myself missing them. These days my favorite way to enjoy bananas is in bread. I have written several banana bread recipes over the years, but this one weaves in a little Asian influence with ground black sesame seeds. If preferred, you can use the seeds whole, which adds a toothsome crunch, or omit them altogether.

MAKES 1 LOAF
VEGAN AND GLUTEN FREE

½ cup (75 g) black sesame seeds

1½ cups (225 g) gluten-free all-purpose flour

2 teaspoons baking powder

½ teaspoon baking soda

5 ripe bananas

½ cup (125 ml) coconut oil

½ cup (125 ml) oat or soy milk

¾ cup (140 g) brown sugar

1 teaspoon vanilla extract

Sea salt

Preheat the oven to 350°F (180°C). Grease and line a standard loaf pan (about 4 x 8 inches / 10 x 20 cm) with parchment paper.

Place the sesame seeds in a blender, small food processor or spice grinder and grind to a powder.

Place the flour, baking powder, baking soda, ground sesame seeds and a pinch of sea salt in a bowl and whisk to combine.

Mash four of the bananas in a separate bowl. Add the coconut oil, milk, brown sugar and vanilla extract and mix well. Fold the banana mixture into the dry ingredients until just combined.

Pour the batter into the prepared pan. Peel the remaining banana and slice in half lengthwise, then lay on top of the batter (this is optional, but it looks pretty). Bake for 50–60 minutes, or until a skewer inserted in the center comes out clean. Allow to cool in the pan for a few minutes, then turn out onto a wire rack. Cut into thick slices and serve warm or at room temperature. Store in an airtight container in the fridge for up to 4 days.

Substitute

Gluten-free flour: all-purpose flour

Black sesame seeds: white sesame seeds or black sesame powder

Oat or soy milk: nondairy milk such as macadamia or coconut

Coconut oil: vegetable or sunflower oil

Peanut and coconut mochi muffins

The texture, the signature chew and the mellow sweetness of these mochi muffins instantly transports me back to childhood, to a crowded dim sum restaurant in Sydney's Chinatown, devouring lo mai chi, a sweet glutinous rice dumpling (see page 243 for my black sesame and coconut mochi recipe). There are many glutinous rice desserts in Asian cuisine, but mochi desserts are definitely the most popular, achieving cross-over into Western culture in the form of ice creams and chewy cakes. Chinese lo mai chi and Japanese daifuku are often filled with red azuki bean paste, but one of my favorite fillings is peanut and coconut, which is the flavor inspiration for these muffins.

Because they are so moreish—meaning you'll definitely want more—I've deliberately made this a big-batch recipe—24 muffins. By all means halve the recipe if you want to, though I can easily eat two or three in one sitting. The muffins also freeze well and can be warmed up in the microwave or oven.

MAKES 24
GLUTEN FREE

1 stick (8 tablespoons / 115 g) unsalted butter, melted and cooled

1 (13.5-ounce / 398 ml) can coconut milk

1 (14-ounce / 396 g) can sweetened condensed milk

4 large eggs, at room temperature

3 cups (425 g) glutinous rice flour

2 teaspoons baking powder

1 cup (185 g) brown sugar

1 cup (60 g) shredded coconut

1 cup (250 g) peanut butter, stirred to loosen up

Combine the butter, coconut milk and condensed milk in a bowl. Break one egg into the mixture at a time, whisking well after each addition.

In a separate bowl, combine the rice flour, baking powder, brown sugar and shredded coconut.

Add the dry ingredients to the milk mixture a few tablespoons at a time, whisking well between additions to prevent lumps (the mixture should look like pancake batter, not too runny or thick). Drop in the peanut butter, a tablespoon at a time, and give it a gentle stir (you don't need to mix the peanut butter completely into the batter—just swirling it through is fine). Let the batter rest for 20 minutes.

Preheat the oven to 350°F (180°C). Generously spray two 12-hole muffin pans with cooking oil.

Spoon the batter into the muffin pans and bake for 30–35 minutes until the muffins are golden. Enjoy warm or at room temperature. Store in an airtight container for up to 3 days, or freeze for up to 3 months.

Veganize

Sweetened condensed milk: coconut condensed milk

Butter: vegan butter

Flourless soy sauce brownies

MAKES 12–16
GLUTEN FREE

1 stick (8 tablespoons / 115 g) unsalted butter

1 cup (175 g) semisweet or dark chocolate bits

1 cup (100 g) almond meal

3 tablespoons cocoa powder

½ teaspoon baking powder

3 large eggs

1 cup (185 g) brown sugar

2 teaspoons vanilla extract

3–4 teaspoons tamari or gluten-free soy sauce

A few years ago I posted a recipe for Vegemite brownies on my website, which raised some eyebrows. Yes, the use of this yeasty, uber-umami sandwich spread in a brownie is surprising, but it brings a complex depth of flavor that is quite unique. These soy sauce brownies are of a similar ilk—where salt is widely used to amplify the "chocolatey" flavors in desserts, soy sauce brings a rich caramel glow. The taste very much resembles salted caramel.

This brownie is gluten free, by way of nutty almond meal and a gluten-free soy sauce. There are many different gluten-free soy sauces on the market and they all work well in this recipe.

Preheat the oven to 350°F (180°C). Grease and line a 9-inch (22.5 cm) square baking pan.

Place the butter and chocolate in a large glass bowl (one that is completely dry and clean) and set over a saucepan of simmering water (do not let the base of the bowl touch the water). Leave until melted, then whisk until smooth. Remove from the heat and allow to cool for 5 minutes.

In another bowl, whisk together the almond meal, cocoa powder and baking powder.

In a third bowl, whisk together the eggs, brown sugar, vanilla extract and soy sauce.

Slowly whisk the egg mixture into the cooled chocolate mixture until well combined. Fold in the dry ingredients.

Pour the batter into the prepared pan and bake for 25 minutes. Remove and allow to cool completely in the pan (I like to leave it in the fridge overnight which makes it easier to handle). Cut into 12–16 pieces (depending on how big you like them). Store in an airtight container in the fridge for up to 1 week.

Substitute

Tamari or soy sauce: 1½ tablespoons Vegemite or 2 teaspoons sea salt flakes

Almond meal: hazelnut meal or ground walnuts

Matcha chia puddings

While matcha green tea rituals have been an important part of Japanese culture for centuries, and were originally used by monks to center themselves during meditation, only recently has the world adopted this antioxidant-rich drink as an everyday beverage. While in Kyoto, we took the kids to a local teahouse where we sipped on hot bowls of slightly bitter matcha, brightened with mouthfuls of wagashi (traditional Japanese sweets). The experience was serene and considered, and nothing like the fast coffee-shop matcha that I usually consume.

This dessert is so simple, relying on the proficient "gelling" powers of chia seeds to turn your matcha-flavored milk into a pudding.

A note: matcha does contain caffeine, which is released steadily and slowly into your system. If you are sensitive to caffeine, switch things up and eat this for breakfast, topped with a dollop of creamy Greek yogurt. Or if caffeine is no issue, swap the matcha for cocoa powder for a satisfying chocolately treat.

SERVES 4
VEGAN AND GLUTEN FREE

2 cups (500 ml) oat milk (or your favorite nut milk)

3 tablespoons maple syrup, or more to taste

2 teaspoons matcha powder, plus extra to serve

¾ cup (130 g) chia seeds

Vegan vanilla ice cream, to serve

Chopped berries, mango, peach or lychees, for topping

Place the milk, maple syrup and matcha powder in a deep bowl and whisk vigorously to dissolve the matcha powder. Add the chia seeds and whisk again.

Pour the chia mixture into a wide-necked jar, then place in the fridge to chill for 30 minutes. Whisk the mixture again to break up any clumps and put it back in the fridge. Chill for at least 3 hours, preferably overnight.

To serve, spoon the pudding into glasses or small bowls and top with a scoop of ice cream and your chosen fruit. Finish with a very light dusting of matcha powder on top.

Substitute

Oat milk: whole or low-fat milk or coconut milk

Maple syrup: honey or brown sugar

Ice cream: Greek yogurt, crème fraîche or whipped cream

Orange chiffon cake

Coming from a family of non-bakers, there was no cake for me when I was growing up. Sweet treats came from nature (fruit), or sometimes from a can (lychees or grass jelly). Once in a while, one of my mum's friends would bring over a slice of pandan chiffon cake. Light as a feather, delicately green and not too sweet (of course), the cakes were an unfamiliar yet decadent after-school treat. Chiffon cake is much like angel cake (it's made using the same cake pan), and is one of the most popular cakes in Asia. It comes in various flavors—from pandan to matcha and chocolate—with an airy, cottony texture and a mellow sweetness that doesn't overpower. This is an orange-scented chiffon cake, an homage to the oranges my dad ate after every meal, and the fruit that Chinese restaurants serve as a final course. I also love the fact that in Chinese custom, the round shape and golden hue of oranges symbolize fullness and wealth.

SERVES 10–12

2 cups (300 g) cake flour (see Note)

3 teaspoons baking powder

½ teaspoon sea salt

7 large eggs, separated

1 cup (230 g) superfine sugar

Zest and juice of 2 oranges (you'll need ¾ cup / 185 ml of juice)

⅓ cup (80 ml) vegetable oil

Confectioners' sugar, for dusting

Preheat the oven to 350°F (180°C). Lightly oil the base of an angel food cake pan (do not oil the side or the middle spout). Alternatively, oil the base of an 8-inch (20 cm) springform cake pan.

In a bowl, whisk together the flour, baking powder and salt.

Place the egg whites in the bowl of a stand mixer (or use a hand-held mixer), add 3 tablespoons of the superfine sugar and beat on high speed until stiff peaks form. Carefully spoon the meringue into a bowl, trying not to knock any of the air out.

In a clean bowl, beat the egg yolks and remaining superfine sugar on high speed until pale and fluffy. Turn the mixer down to low. Add the orange zest, then slowly trickle in the orange juice, followed by the oil, and beat until combined.

Using a large metal spoon, fold the flour mixture into the egg yolk mixture, a few tablespoons at a time, until it has all been incorporated. Gently fold in the egg whites.

Carefully pour the batter into the prepared pan and bake for 45 minutes. Allow the cake to cool in the angel food cake pan, upside down on a wire rack—the cake will stick to the side, it won't fall out! (If you are using a springform pan, let it cool in the pan for a few minutes, then turn it out onto a wire rack.) When completely cool, run a thin offset spatula along the side to loosen the cake, then carefully unmold it. Cut into slices and dust with confectioners' sugar. Tightly wrap any leftover cake in plastic wrap or foil (to prevent it from drying out) and store in the fridge for up to 5 days.

Note: Cake flour has slightly less protein than all-purpose flour (protein turns to gluten, which makes cakes chewy and tough—you get my drift, right?). To make your own cake flour at home, take 1 cup (150 g) of all-purpose flour, then replace 2 tablespoons of the flour with 2 tablespoons of cornstarch.

Substitute

Orange: lemon, lime or passion fruit

Sago pudding with passion fruit caramel

Sago is made with the starch from the pith of sago palm trees. The white balls are neutral in flavor, with the distinct slippery mouthfeel that is common in starchy foods. While it's an unusual ingredient, sago puddings and jellies are actually very easy to prepare, often paired with coconut milk and topped with tropical fruits such as mango, pineapple or melon. In this recipe, I've given this popular Asian dessert some flair with a dazzling passion fruit caramel. Passion fruit is one of my favorite fruit flavors, but it can be very hard to find it fresh in New York, so I always make sure my pantry is well stocked with canned passion fruit from Australia (the size of the small cans is just perfect!). Certain desserts, like pavlova for example, simply cannot be eaten without passion fruit pulp.

This passion fruit caramel is a revelation—it's more tangy than sweet, and it's also perfect ladled over vanilla ice cream, or even on top of pavlova.

SERVES 4
VEGAN AND GLUTEN FREE

1 cup (195 g) small sago pearls

1 (13.5-ounce / 398 ml) can unsweetened coconut cream

3 tablespoons superfine sugar

½ teaspoon vanilla extract

Passion fruit caramel

⅓ cup (80 g) superfine sugar

6 ounces (170 g) passion fruit pulp (fresh or canned)

Bring a large saucepan of water to the boil, then reduce the heat to medium and add the sago. Cook for 10–12 minutes, stirring often, until the sago is transparent. Drain and set aside.

Set aside 1 tablespoon of coconut cream for the passion fruit caramel and 2 tablespoons for serving.

For the passion fruit caramel, place a saucepan over high heat. Add the superfine sugar and 2 tablespoons of water and stir until the sugar has dissolved, about 2–3 minutes. As soon as the liquid turns a light amber color, reduce the heat to low and add the passion fruit pulp and reserved 1 tablespoon of coconut cream. Cook, stirring, for 1 minute or so, until bubbly and thick.

Pour the remaining coconut cream into a saucepan, add the superfine sugar, vanilla extract and ½ cup (125 ml) of water. Stir over medium–low heat for 2 minutes until well combined, then remove from the heat. Pour the coconut cream mixture over the sago and stir well.

Ladle the sago pudding into bowls and top with spoonfuls of the passion fruit caramel. Finish with a drizzle of the reserved coconut cream. This sago pudding can be served warm, cold or at room temperature. The longer it sits the more it will solidify, like jelly.

Substitute

Sago: tapioca balls

Coconut cream: cream

Black sesame and coconut mochi

MAKES 12–14
VEGAN AND GLUTEN FREE

1 cup (150 g) glutinous rice flour
(sweet rice flour)

¾ cup (170 g) superfine sugar

Cornstarch, for dusting

⅔ cup (60 g) shredded coconut

Black sesame and coconut filling

½ cup (75 g) black sesame seeds

1 tablespoon superfine sugar

3 tablespoons coconut cream

1 tablespoon shredded coconut

Pinch of sea salt

Mochi (as they call them in Japan) have experienced a surge in popularity in recent years and are now widely available filled with ice cream, but when I was growing up I knew them as lo mai chi (in Cantonese)—sticky balls filled with either red bean paste or peanuts with coconut. They were, and still are, one of my favorite desserts from the sweets trolley at dim sum. Mochi balls have a soft, squishy consistency that is a signature of most things made with glutinous rice flour. Making homemade mochi may seem daunting, but it's actually quite simple. You just need the confidence to work with a dough that is unfathomably stretchy and sticky. Dust your hands generously with cornstarch and work quickly and assertively. And don't worry if they look a little wonky—they will still taste amazing.

For the black sesame and coconut filling, place the sesame seeds in a dry frying pan and toast over low heat for 4–5 minutes until aromatic, shaking the pan every now and then. Place the seeds and superfine sugar in a blender or food processor and blend until finely ground. Pour the ground seeds into a bowl, add the remaining ingredients and stir to form a thick paste.

Whisk together the glutinous rice flour and 1¼ cups (310 ml) of water until the flour has dissolved. Pour the mixture through a sieve into a saucepan. Stir in the superfine sugar, then place over medium heat and stir continuously for about 3 minutes until you have a very sticky dough ball. Remove from the heat.

Lay a sheet of parchment paper on a cutting board and sprinkle generously with cornstarch. Tip the dough ball onto the paper and allow to cool slightly before sprinkling with more cornstarch. Cut the dough into 12–14 pieces.

Sprinkle the shredded coconut onto a plate.

Dust your hands with a little cornstarch before handling the sticky dough. Roll a piece into a ball, then flatten into a disc using your hands and fingers. The dough should be soft and malleable. Place about 1 teaspoon of the black sesame filling in the center, then pull the sides up and over the filling, pinching and twisting to seal the dough. Roll the ball in the shredded coconut to coat, and reshape the ball if you need to. If you find that your hands are feeling sticky, just dust again with cornstarch. Repeat with the remaining dough and filling.

Mochi are best eaten immediately. They can be left in an airtight container at room temperature for 24 hours only. Avoid storing them in the fridge as they will harden. If you have leftover mochi, freeze and then consume them frozen.

Substitute

Black sesame seeds: white sesame
seeds or peanuts

Cornstarch: potato starch

Acknowledgments

This book is rooted in the smell of ginger on my mother's hands. Thank you to my mum, who was born Lee Yuk Ling, later became Yuk Ling Lui, and then Lindy. She has lived many lives, and like many immigrants, has experienced challenges that I will never quite understand. But still, she was one of the lucky ones, and through it all she has dedicated her life to her children. Thank you for every big breakfast, every bowl of macaroni soup and every plate of perfectly steamed savory egg custard. Mum, I remember it all.

Thank you to my dad. Wai Keung Lui, who later became Ken. He was a big personality with a commanding voice that belied his gentle nature. He paved the way for our family to make a new life in Australia, a man who worked several jobs but never once complained. I don't speak about him enough because I fear my memories will not do him justice. But Dad, you are remembered.

Thank you to my siblings, Letty and Kerby, who have quietly supported me over the years by holding down the fort at home while I errantly made my way in the world.

Enduring thanks to my incredible family at Plum. Thank you Mary Small, for the unwavering trust you show in my work; your belief in *my way* allows me to tell my stories with ultimate truth. I am indebted to Clare Marshall for making work seem like play. Thank you to my dear friend Charlotte Ree, who invented the phrase "above and beyond." Thank you to the extended Pan Macmillan team, the incredible sales team who knock on doors and support me and my books in the field. Thank you to Daniel New who approaches each book design like it's a piece of art—I'm always just so honored to work with you. Thank you also to Allie Schotte and Rachel Carter.

Thank you to my US publishing family at Prestel. From Germany to the UK, to the US, I am truly grateful for your support and dedication to bringing my stories to the world. Thank you to Holly La Due, your friendship and support over the years has meant so much to me. And gratitude to my editor Lauren Salkeld who has endured hours of trying to decipher my Aussie vernacular. Thank you also to Anjali Pala.

Thank you to my agent, Judy Linden, for being my voice of reason, my rock, my friend.

Thank you to Photoworks SF, who, during the Summer of 2019, efficiently and diligently processed and scanned rolls and rolls of film. I am truly grateful for the care you took in every single photo.

Thank you to my friend and colleague Shirley Cai, who is the little sister I never had, but also one of the cleverest people I know. I hope to be just like you when I grow up.

Thank you to Maria Midoes and Leetal Arazi, who are as essential to me as my daily coffee—I am so grateful for your friendship, which always brings sanity, honesty and laughter to my days. Thank you to Davida Sweeney, Jennifer Wong and Samantha Hillman, who never fail to bring humor and wit to my life.

A big thank you from my heart to all the home cooks who have so steadfastly cooked from my books, food columns, Instagram feed and website over the years—you guys are truly my heroes. I owe you all so much for creating a community in food that is stronger than I could have ever imagined. Thank you also to the bookstores and specialty stores, big and small, who continue to show so much love and support for my books.

Of course, thank you to my little family, my motley crew, who are everything I need in life. To my daughter Scout, my bright star, Dash, my brilliant moon, and Huck, my gentle sun—you guys fill my days with brightness, purpose and joy. To my husband Ross, who has, for several decades, made my life more rad.

– Hetty Lui McKinnon 雷瑜

Index

© 2021 Hetty McKinnon

Originally published by Pan Macmillan Australia Pty Limited, 2020

Prestel Verlag, Munich · London · New York 2021
A member of Penguin Random House Verlagsgruppe GmbH
Neumarkter Strasse 28 · 81673 Munich
Second edition, 2021

Text copyright © Hetty McKinnon 2020
Photographs © Hetty McKinnon 2020, except images on pages 8, 74–75,
108, 110–111 copyright © Shirley Cai 2020

Design Daniel New copyright © 2020

Library of Congress Control Number: 2020945730
A CIP catalogue record for this book is available from the British Library.

For Pan Macmillan:
Design by Daniel New
Edited by Rachel Carter
Index by Helena Holmgren
Photography by Hetty McKinnon,
with additional photography by Shirley Cai
Food and prop styling by Hetty McKinnon
Typeset by Daniel New and Hannah Schubert

For Prestel:
Editorial direction by Holly La Due
Cover design by Anjali Pala
Production by Corinna Pickart
Copyediting by Lauren Salkeld
Proofreading by Monica Parcell
Printing and binding by DZS Grafik, d.o.o., Ljubljana

Printed in Slovenia

Penguin Random House Verlagsgruppe FSC©N001967

ISBN 978-3-7913-8683-6

www.prestel.com

HETTY McKINNON is a cook and food writer with a passion for vegetables. In 2011, she established Arthur Street Kitchen, a local salad-delivery business run out of her home in Sydney, Australia. In 2015, Hetty and her family relocated to Brooklyn, New York, where she continues to cook and write about food.

As well as her genre-defining debut *Community*, Hetty is the author of two bestselling cookbooks: *Neighborhood* and the award-winning *Family*. She is also the editor and publisher of food journal *Peddler* and hosts its podcast The House Specials. Her recipes and writing can be found in the *New York Times*, *Bon Appetit*, *Epicurious*, *Food & Wine* and *The Guardian*.

arthurstreetkitchen.com